THE GOSPEL

GOD'S PLAN for PRESCHOOLERS

While preschoolers might not be ready to respond to the gospel, use this guide to help little minds begin to grasp big truths about Jesus and the kingdom of God.

GOD IS KING.

Ask: "Who is in charge at home? Who is in charge over the whole world?" Explain that God made everything! He is King over everything, and He is in charge.

WE SINNED.

Ask: "Have you ever done something wrong?" Tell preschoolers that everyone sins, or disobeys God. Our sin makes God sad.

GOD SENT JESUS.

Explain that God must punish sin. He loves us and He sent His Son, Jesus, to earth. Jesus came to take away the punishment for sin.

JESUS LOVES.

Ask: "Do you like presents?" Explain that Jesus gives us the best present. He never did anything wrong, but He was punished in our place. Jesus wants to take away our sin because He loves us.

Pray that God will save your preschoolers. As you faithfully teach the Bible, you are planting gospel seeds in children's hearts. Ask God to grow the preschoolers into children who love and trust in Jesus.

Bible Study
at a Glance

Start here

Leader Bible Study

Familiarize yourself with the content and context of the Bible story and how it relates to God's plan of redemption.

Preparation

Pray for your preschoolers and contact families during the week. Gather and prepare session materials.

Pray for your preschoolers

Send a parent e-mail

Print/download printables

Assemble supplies

Prepare videos

Activity Page

Opening Activities

Introduce the Story

Engage preschoolers and introduce the day's Bible story.

Say what?
Use the suggested "Say" dialogue to easily move between segments.

Tell the Story

Communicate the day's Bible story and discover God's big story.

Bible Story

Giant Timeline

Big Picture Question

Key Passage

Sing

Suggested times
The times provided allow you to complete the session plan in an hour. Lengthen or shorten the session as needed.

Make it fit

 1 room

1) Use "Introduce the Story" to welcome preschoolers to Bible study. Preschoolers may work the activity page and/or complete an activity together.
2) Transition to an area within your classroom that can be designated as the "Tell the Story" area. Watch the Bible story video or tell the Bible story. Incorporate any large group elements that fit your space and your time constraints.
3) Regroup to the "Experience the Story" area by using a countdown video. Set up activities in one of these ways: as a group, all at the same time; in small groups that rotate through each activity; set up as centers, allowing preschoolers to browse and choose.

1 or more rooms

1) Use "Introduce the Story" to welcome preschoolers to Bible study. Preschoolers may work the activity page and/or complete an activity together.
2) Use the countdown video or other transition signal as you move your small group to join the other small groups in the "Tell the Story" area. Watch the Bible story video or tell the Bible story. Incorporate any large group elements that fit your space and your time constraints.
3) Regroup to the "Experience the Story" area where you will reinforce what preschoolers learned from the "Tell the Story" leader. Set up activities in one of these ways: as a group, all at the same time; in small groups that rotate through each activity; set up as centers, allowing preschoolers to browse and choose.

Activities

Experience the Story

Snack & Transition

Reinforce the Bible Story by engaging in fun activities for multiple learning styles.

Check out our tips and resources for an additional hour in the Worship Guide!

Unit 28: The God Who Empowers

Unit Description:
After Jesus returned to heaven, the Holy Spirit—whom He had promised to send—was given to the disciples. Filled with the Holy Spirit's power, the small group of disciples shared the gospel and the early church grew rapidly.

Key Passage:
Philippians 2:13

Big Picture Question:
What does the Holy Spirit do? The Holy Spirit helps Christians.

Unit 28: The God Who Empowers

Session 1:
Bible Story:
The Holy Spirit Came
Bible Passage:
Acts 2:1-4,22-42
Main Point:
The Holy Spirit came to Jesus' followers.

Session 2:
Bible Story:
Peter Healed a Beggar
Bible Passage:
Acts 3:1-10; 4:5-31
Main Point:
In Jesus' name, Peter healed a man.

Session 3:
Bible Story:
Stephen's Address
Bible Passage:
Acts 6:8–7:60
Main Point:
Stephen told people about Jesus, even when he would be hurt for it.

Session 4:
Bible Story:
The Ethiopian Official Believed
Bible Passage:
Acts 8:26-40
Main Point:
Philip told the Ethiopian man about Jesus.

Session 5:
Bible Story:
Peter Visited Cornelius
Bible Passage:
Acts 10
Main Point:
Peter learned the gospel is for all people.

The Holy Spirit Came

1

BIBLE PASSAGE: Acts 2:1-4,22-42

MAIN POINT: The Holy Spirit came to Jesus' followers.

KEY PASSAGE: Philippians 2:13

BIG PICTURE QUESTION: What does the Holy Spirit do? The Holy Spirit helps Christians.

INTRODUCE THE STORY
(15–20 MINUTES)
PAGE 10

→

TELL THE STORY
(10–15 MINUTES)
PAGE 12

→

EXPERIENCE THE STORY
(20–25 MINUTES)
PAGE 14

Leader BIBLE STUDY

When Jesus ascended to heaven, He instructed the disciples to go to Jerusalem and wait. Jesus promised that the Holy Spirit would come upon them. So the disciples went back to Jerusalem, where they waited and prayed.

The time came for the Jewish festival called Pentecost, or the Feast of Weeks. As with the Passover festival, Jews from all over the Roman Empire would be at the temple in Jerusalem.

During this festival, the Holy Spirit came to believers in Jerusalem. They heard a sound like a violent, rushing wind. When the Holy Spirit filled the disciples, they were able to speak in foreign languages. They went out into the city and began to preach, and the Jews from all over the world were amazed. These disciples were from Galilee, but they were speaking in languages the visitors could understand.

The disciples told people about God's plan. The Holy Spirit helped Peter teach: Jesus is the Messiah; Jesus was killed, but He is alive! (Acts 2:22-36) The Holy Spirit convicted the crowd and they asked, "Brothers, what must we do?" Peter told them to repent and be baptized in the name of Jesus. (Acts 2:37-38) That day, three thousand people received salvation!

God kept His promise to send the Holy Spirit. With the Holy Spirit's help, Jesus' disciples could share the gospel with the entire world.

God gives the Holy Spirit to those who trust in Jesus as Lord and Savior. As you teach preschoolers, emphasize that the Holy Spirit gives us power to do God's work, and He changes us to be more like Jesus.

Check out the video "The Big Story" for a picture of this quarter's part in God's big story of redemption.

1

MINISTRY GRID
training made simple

Additional resources for each session are available at *gospelproject.com*. For free training and session-by-session help, visit *www.ministrygrid.com/web/thegospelproject*.

The BIBLE STORY

Bible Storytelling Tips

The Holy Spirit Came
Acts 2:1-4,22-42

- **Use sound effects:** Locate sound effects for a strong, rushing wind; other languages; and water splash (for people being baptized). Play the sound effects at appropriate moments in the Bible story.

- **Tell the Bible story in another language:** Invite a guest who speaks another language to tell the Bible story to your class. Ask the guest to tell the Bible story in English and then in the other language. Encourage them to use the same hand motions, tone, and facial expressions in each storytelling.

People came from far away to the city of Jerusalem for the feast of Pentecost. **Jesus' friends were meeting together. All of a sudden, a sound like a strong, rushing wind came from heaven and filled the whole house. The Holy Spirit filled the friends.** When they started talking, they sounded different. **They could speak in languages they didn't even know!**

Other Jews in Jerusalem came to see what was going on. The **people** were **from many nations**; they spoke different languages. But all of them **could understand what Jesus' friends were saying!**

Peter stood up to talk to the crowd. "You saw the miracles Jesus did," he said. "God planned for Jesus to die. Then God raised Jesus from the dead! Now, Jesus is sitting beside God in heaven, and He sent the Holy Spirit to us."

Then **Peter said, "Jesus is the Lord and Messiah! You killed Him on a cross!"**

The people knew Peter was telling the truth. "What should we do?" they asked.

"Turn away from your sins and be baptized," Peter said. "God will forgive your sins, and you will get the Holy Spirit too."

That day, **three thousand people** turned away from their sins and were baptized. They all **believed and became followers of Jesus.**

Christ Connection: God sent the Holy Spirit just as He promised. Now Jesus' friends had everything they needed to make more followers of Jesus! God gives the Holy Spirit to those of us who trust in Jesus. The Holy Spirit helps us do God's work and changes us to be more like Jesus.

WANT TO DISCOVER GOD'S WORD? GET *MORE!*

Invite preschoolers to check out this week's devotionals to discover how God's Word can help them grow in the gospel. Order in bulk, subscribe quarterly, or purchase individually. For more information, check out *www.lifeway.com/ devotionals.*

Introduce THE STORY

SESSION TITLE: The Holy Spirit Came
BIBLE PASSAGE: Acts 2:1-4,22-42
MAIN POINT: The Holy Spirit came to Jesus' followers.
KEY PASSAGE: Philippians 2:13
BIG PICTURE QUESTION: What does the Holy Spirit do? The Holy Spirit helps Christians.

Welcome time

- "The Story" song
- offering basket
- Allergy Alert download
- favorite toys related to the Bible story theme

Play the unit theme song in the background as you greet preschoolers and follow your church's security procedures. Set an offering basket near the door to collect at an appropriate time. Post an allergy alert, if necessary. Set out a few favorite theme-related toys, such as puzzles and blocks.

Activity page

- "Count the People" activity page, 1 per child
- pencils or crayons

Invite preschoolers to fill in the correct number in each blank.

SAY • Look at all the people you counted! In today's Bible story, many people turned away from their sin and followed Jesus. Listen closely to discover just how many there were.

Play a waiting game

- paper
- scissors
- marker
- ball

Write the numbers *1–10* on strips of paper. Guide children to sit in a circle. Fan the strips, keeping the numbers hidden from preschoolers. Allow a child to draw a strip of paper and reveal the number. Give him a small ball. He must hold the ball until the class has counted to the number he drew. Lead the children in counting, and then instruct the child to roll the ball to another preschooler. Then that preschooler may draw a strip. Continue play until each preschooler has had a turn.

SAY • Was it hard to wait until we finished counting to roll the ball? Waiting can be hard. In today's Bible story, Jesus' friends were waiting. Before Jesus left earth and returned to heaven, He promised to send the Holy Spirit to His friends. He told them to wait in Jerusalem. The friends were meeting together in Jerusalem when the Holy Spirit came.

Make a windsock

Before the session, cut streamers into 2-foot lengths. Invite preschoolers to decorate a sheet of construction paper. Lead preschoolers to turn the paper over and tape steamers along the bottom edge of their paper. Form the construction paper into a cylinder and use tape to secure it in place. Punch holes on opposite sites of the top of the cylinder. Tie yarn through the holes to form a handle.

- construction paper
- tape
- crepe paper streamers
- hole punch
- yarn
- scissors
- markers or crayons

SAY • You can hang your windsock outside and watch the streamers flap in the wind. In today's Bible story, Jesus' friends were meeting together when they heard a sound like a strong, rushing wind that came from heaven and filled the whole house. Listen to hear what happened next.

Transition to tell the story

To gain the attention of all the preschoolers to move them to Bible study, show the countdown video, flip off the lights, or clap a simple rhythm for the children to copy. Challenge preschoolers to pretend to be the wind as they move to Bible study by waving their arms in the air and making whooshing sounds.

- countdown video (optional)

Tell THE STORY

SESSION TITLE: The Holy Spirit Came
BIBLE PASSAGE: Acts 2:1-4,22-42
MAIN POINT: The Holy Spirit came to Jesus' followers.
KEY PASSAGE: Philippians 2:13
BIG PICTURE QUESTION: What does the Holy Spirit do? The Holy Spirit helps Christians.

Introduce the Bible story

Tip: Use an online translation tool that allows you to hear the proper pronunciation.

Before the session, practice saying "Welcome to Bible study today" in another language. Say the phrase to preschoolers several times before translating for them.

SAY • Did you understand what I said? You do not speak [*language*], so you could not understand. In today's Bible story, the Holy Spirit made Jesus' friends able to speak in languages they did not even know.

Watch or tell the Bible story

• Bible
• bookmark
• "The Holy Spirit Came" video
• Bible Story Picture Poster

Place a bookmark at Acts 2 in your Bible. Invite a preschooler to open it. Reverently display the open Bible.

SAY • The Bible is the most important book there is. The Bible has God's words in it. All God's words are true. Today's Bible story is from Acts in the New Testament. Show the video or tell the Bible story using the provided storytelling helps. Use the bolded version of the Bible story for young preschoolers.

Talk about the Bible story

• Main Point Poster
• Giant Timeline or Big Story Circle

SAY • **The Holy Spirit came to Jesus' followers** just as Jesus promised. The Holy Spirit helped Jesus' friends tell people from many nations the good news about

Jesus. Three thousand people became followers of
Jesus in just one day!

Point to the Bible story picture on the giant timeline or big
story circle as you ask the following review questions:

1. Who came to Jesus' friends just as He promised? (*the
   Holy Spirit*)
2. How were the friends able to speak in languages they
   did not know? (*The Holy Spirit gave them power.*)
3. Who told the crowd that Jesus is the Messiah? (*Peter*)
4. What did Peter say would happen if the people
   turned away from their sins and were baptized? (*God
   would forgive their sin and give them the Holy Spirit.*)

Learn the big picture question

SAY • Our big picture question asks, ***What does the Holy
Spirit do? The Holy Spirit helps Christians.*** The
Holy Spirit helped Jesus' friends share the good news
with people from many different nations. God gives
the Holy Spirit to everyone who trusts in Jesus. The
Holy Spirit helps us do God's work and changes us
to be more like Jesus.

• Big Picture Question
  Poster

Practice the key passage

Open your Bible to Philippians 2:13. Read the key passage
aloud several times. Sing together the key passage song,
"Working in You."

• Key Passage Poster
• "Working in You" song

SAY • Obeying God and doing His work are not things
we can do on our own. We are sinners, but our key
passage reminds us that God works in us to help us
obey Him and do the work He has for us.

Transition to experience the story

Experience THE STORY

SESSION TITLE: The Holy Spirit Came

BIBLE PASSAGE: Acts 2:1-4,22-42

MAIN POINT: The Holy Spirit came to Jesus' followers.

KEY PASSAGE: Philippians 2:13

BIG PICTURE QUESTION: What does the Holy Spirit do? The Holy Spirit helps Christians.

Learn the key passage

Invite preschoolers to repeat the key passage after you while you teach them simple hand motions for each phrase. Use the following motions or create your own. Adjust the text of the verse to fit the version of the Bible you are using.

It is God [*Lift hands to heaven.*]

who is working in you [*Point toward self with thumbs.*]

according to His good purpose [*Lift hands to heaven.*]

Philippians 2:13 [*Hold hands together like an open book.*]

Repeat multiple times until the children are comfortable with the hand motions.

SAY • Our key passage reminds us that God is working in us and through us by the Holy Spirit. **The Holy Spirit came to Jesus' followers** just as He promised. God gives the Holy Spirit to those of us who trust in Jesus. The Holy Spirit helps us do God's work and changes us to be more like Jesus. *What does the Holy Spirit do? The Holy Spirit helps Christians.*

Make play dough people

- play dough
- people-shaped cookie cutters (optional)

Set out play dough. Invite preschoolers to make as many people figures as they can out of play dough. Consider providing people-shaped cookie cutters. Periodically count how many people preschoolers have made.

SAY • You made many people, but even more people than this became followers of Jesus in today's Bible story. **The Holy Spirit came to Jesus' followers** and gave them power to preach the good news. Peter told the crowd that Jesus is the Messiah. The people knew Peter was telling the truth. Three thousand people turned away from their sin and followed Jesus that day.

Sing "Jesus Loves Me" in another language

Before the session, look online to learn how to sing "Jesus Loves Me" in another language or use the provided lyrics. Teach preschoolers how to sing the song. Alternate singing the song in English and the other language you chose. Consider inviting to class a church member who speaks another language to teach the song to your group.

• "Jesus Loves Me Lyrics" printable (optional)
• guest (optional)

SAY • You sang the good news about Jesus in another language. When **the Holy Spirit came to Jesus' followers**, they were able to speak in other languages. They did not have to learn or practice! Many people heard the good news about Jesus and believed. God gives the Holy Spirit to those who trust in Jesus. The Holy Spirit helps us do God's work and changes us to be more like Jesus.

Match sounds

Gather different materials that will fit inside plastic eggs or identical, opaque containers while allowing some movement. Fill two eggs with each material. Seal the eggs with tape.

Invite preschoolers to shake each egg and listen to the

• plastic eggs or small, opaque containers
• masking tape
• various materials: dried beans, rice, coins, marbles, popcorn kernels, beads, buttons, pebbles, water beads
• marker (optional)

The God Who Empowers

sound it makes. Invite preschoolers to find the egg with the matching sound. Consider placing identical materials in the same color egg for younger preschoolers or label containers with matching numbers or letters. When preschoolers are finished matching, allow them to guess each egg's contents.

SAY • When you shook the eggs, did you recognize the sounds? In today's Bible story, people from many nations recognized their own languages when Jesus' followers spoke. **The Holy Spirit came to Jesus' followers.** God gives the Holy Spirit to those of us who trust in Jesus. The Holy Spirit helps us do God's work and changes us to be more like Jesus.

Create wind

• straws
• masking tape
• various objects: feathers, cotton balls, pom-poms, table tennis balls, pieces of string

Tip: Choose objects that will not fit through a straw.

Give each preschooler a straw. Use masking tape to create a starting line and a finish line on opposite ends of a table. Place an object on the table at the starting line. Invite a preschooler to use her straw to blow the object to the finish line. Allow preschoolers to take turns blowing objects with their straws.

SAY • Jesus' friends were meeting together when they heard a sound like a strong, rushing wind. **The Holy Spirit came to Jesus' followers.** God sent the Holy Spirit just as He promised. Now Jesus' friends had everything they needed to make more followers of Jesus! When we put our trust in Jesus, God gives us the Holy Spirit too.

Snack

Play the countdown video to signal the end of activities. Guide preschoolers to clean their areas. Take a restroom break and wash hands. Gather preschoolers for snack time. Thank God for the snack.

Serve filled donuts or cupcakes for snack. Talk about how **the Holy Spirit came to Jesus' followers.** Jesus' friends were filled with the Holy Spirit. Remark that you cannot see the Holy Spirit in a person like you can see the filling in the donut or the cupcake. But we can know that Holy Spirit is in a person when we see that person becoming more like Jesus in his thoughts and actions.

- countdown video (optional)
- Allergy Alert download
- snack food
- paper cups and napkins

Transition

When a child finishes his snack, guide him to throw away any trash. He may select a book or puzzle to examine, play quietly with play dough or a favorite toy, or color the Bible story coloring page.

Offer the journal page and invite preschoolers to fill their paper with drawings of people. Remind preschoolers that three thousand people followed Jesus in one day. Explain that when a person turns away from his or her sin and follows Jesus, God gives that person the Holy Spirit.

SAY • God, thank You for giving us the Holy Spirit when we turn away from our sin and put our trust in Jesus. Thank You, Holy Spirit, for changing us to be more like Jesus and helping us do God's work. Amen.

If parents are picking up their children at this time, tell them something that their child enjoyed doing or did well during the session. Distribute the preschool big picture cards for families.

- books
- puzzles
- play dough
- Journal Page printable, 1 per child
- Bible Story Coloring Page
- crayons
- *Big Picture Cards for Families: Babies, Toddlers, and Preschoolers*

Peter Healed a Beggar

BIBLE PASSAGE: Acts 3:1-10; 4:5-31

MAIN POINT: In Jesus' name, Peter healed a man.

KEY PASSAGE: Philippians 2:13

BIG PICTURE QUESTION: What does the Holy Spirit do? The Holy Spirit helps Christians.

INTRODUCE THE STORY	TELL THE STORY	EXPERIENCE THE STORY
(15–20 MINUTES)	(10–15 MINUTES)	(20–25 MINUTES)
PAGE 22	PAGE 24	PAGE 26

 → →

Leader BIBLE STUDY

With the coming of the Holy Spirit at Pentecost, Jesus' disciples were empowered to carry out Jesus' mission for them—to take the gospel to all the nations. More and more people believed in Jesus. They met together at the temple to praise and worship God, and the first church began.

One afternoon, two of Jesus' disciples—Peter and John—went to the temple to pray. They encountered at the gate a man who could not walk. Rather than give the man money, Peter gave him something much more valuable: immediate physical healing in Jesus' name.

As you teach this Bible story to preschoolers, keep three things in mind. First, Peter's healing the beggar was not magic; it was a miracle. Beginning in Acts 3:12, Peter responded to the people who were amazed at what had happened. "Why are you amazed at this ... as though we had made him walk by our own power?" The man wasn't healed because Peter was a super-believer. Peter explained that it was by Jesus' power the man was healed.

Second, the man's healing made him happy and thankful. He entered the temple and rejoiced! Consider the wonderful miracle of salvation. We are dead in our sin, and God makes us alive in Christ! How we should rejoice and give thanks to the Lord!

Finally, Peter and John were bold in their witness. When confronted by the religious leaders, they did not shy away. Peter and John preached about the salvation found in Jesus. In fact, they said they were "unable to stop speaking about what we have seen and heard" (Acts 4:20).

The same power that enabled Peter to heal the man who was lame—the power of the Holy Spirit—enables believers today to live on mission for Jesus. Pray that God would give the preschoolers you teach a willingness to be used by Him for His glory and for the fame of Jesus' name.

MINISTRY GRID
training made simple

Additional resources for each session are available at *gospelproject.com.* For free training and session-by-session help, visit *www.ministrygrid.com/web/thegospelproject.*

The BIBLE STORY

Peter Healed a Beggar
Acts 3:1-10; 4:5-31

- **Play it out:** Invite preschoolers to pretend to be the man who could not walk. Invite them to sit down and pretend to ask for money. When you come to the part of the story where the man is healed, invite preschoolers to stand up, jump, and walk around the room praising God.

- **Make it physical:** Guide preschoolers to stand at one end of the room while you tell the Bible story. Invite them to take a step forward every time you say "walk."

One day, **Peter and John went to the temple** to pray. **They saw a man sitting by the gate. The man could not walk, so every day his friends carried him to the temple. As people went into the temple, the man asked them for money** since he could not work.

The man asked Peter and John for help. Peter said to him, "Look at us." The man looked at Peter and John. He thought they were going to give him money.

"I do not have silver or gold," Peter said. But Peter did have something better. **"In the name of Jesus, stand up and walk."**

Peter helped the man up. The man was healed! His feet were strong, and he could walk and jump. Then the man went into the temple with Peter and John, and he praised God.

Everyone who saw the man was amazed. This was the man who could not walk, but now he could walk! How could such a wonderful thing happen?

The next day, the religious leaders met together. They **asked Peter and John, "How did you heal this man?"**

Peter was filled with the Holy Spirit and **said, "This man was healed by the power of Jesus." Then Peter told the religious leaders that Jesus is the most important One of all.**

The religious leaders did not know what to say. They **told Peter and John** to be quiet and **to stop telling people about Jesus.**

But Peter said, "We cannot keep quiet. We must tell people what we have seen and heard." Peter and John met with other believers and prayed that God would give them power to be brave and tell people about Jesus.

Christ Connection: After Jesus went back to heaven, the Holy Spirit gave Jesus' followers power to begin working. With the power of Jesus' name, Peter healed a man who could not walk. The religious leaders could not stop Jesus' followers from telling people the good news about Jesus.

WANT TO DISCOVER GOD'S WORD? GET *MORE!*

Invite preschoolers to check out this week's devotionals to discover how God's Word can help them grow in the gospel. Order in bulk, subscribe quarterly, or purchase individually. For more information, check out *www.lifeway.com/devotionals*.

Introduce THE STORY

SESSION TITLE: Peter Healed a Beggar
BIBLE PASSAGE: Acts 3:1-10; 4:5-31
MAIN POINT: In Jesus' name, Peter healed a man.
KEY PASSAGE: Philippians 2:13
BIG PICTURE QUESTION: What does the Holy Spirit do? The Holy Spirit helps Christians.

Welcome time

- "The Story" song
- offering basket
- Allergy Alert download
- favorite toys related to the Bible story theme

Play the unit theme song in the background as you greet preschoolers and follow your church's security procedures. Set an offering basket near the door to collect at an appropriate time. Post an allergy alert, if necessary. Set out a few favorite theme-related toys, such as puzzles and blocks.

Activity page

- "What Is Different?" activity page, 1 per child
- pencils or crayons

Invite preschoolers to look at the two pictures and circle the seven differences they see in the second picture.

SAY • In today's Bible story, a man could not walk. Peter and John met him as they were going to the temple to pray. The man thought Peter and John would give him money, but Peter did something better. Can you guess what Peter did for the man from the second picture?

Play a quiet game

Guide preschoolers to sit in a line. Choose a child to stand in front of the group and move silly and silently to try to make the other children laugh. The child who is last to laugh gets to go next. If multiple children do not laugh after 30 seconds, choose one of them to go next.

SAY • Staying quiet was hard when your friend was being silly! In today's Bible story, the religious leaders told Peter and John to be quiet and to stop telling people about Jesus. But Peter said, "We cannot keep quiet. We must tell people what we have seen and heard." Listen to hear what happened.

Make a megaphone

Give each preschooler a sheet of paper. Set out markers or crayons and stickers for preschoolers to decorate their paper. When preschoolers are finished decorating their paper, roll it so that one end is small and the other is large to form a megaphone. Tape the paper in place. Show preschoolers how to speak into the small end to amplify their voices.

• paper
• markers or crayons
• stickers
• tape

SAY • You use a megaphone when you want to be loud so many people can hear you. In today's Bible story, Peter and John wanted many people to hear the good news about Jesus, but they did not use a megaphone. Listen to our story to hear how Peter and John shared the good news.

Transition to tell the story

To gain the attention of all the preschoolers to move them to Bible study, show the countdown video, flip off the lights, or clap a simple rhythm for the children to copy. Invite preschoolers to jump to Bible study.

• countdown video (optional)

Tell THE STORY

SESSION TITLE: Peter Healed a Beggar

BIBLE PASSAGE: Acts 3:1-10; 4:5-31

MAIN POINT: In Jesus' name, Peter healed a man.

KEY PASSAGE: Philippians 2:13

BIG PICTURE QUESTION: What does the Holy Spirit do? The Holy Spirit helps Christians.

Introduce the Bible story

Lead preschoolers to march in place, tap their toes, stomp their feet, sit down, and cross their legs.

SAY • In today's Bible story, Peter and John met a man who could not walk. Listen to our Bible story to hear how Peter helped the man.

Watch or tell the Bible story

- Bible
- bookmark
- "Peter Healed a Beggar" video
- Bible Story Picture Poster

Place a bookmark at Acts 3 in your Bible. Invite a preschooler to open it. Reverently display the open Bible.

SAY • God is so kind to give us His words in the Bible. We can believe what God says in the Bible because His words are true. Today's Bible story is in Acts.

Show the video or tell the Bible story using the provided storytelling helps. Use the bolded version of the Bible story for young preschoolers.

Talk about the Bible story

- Main Point Poster
- Giant Timeline or Big Story Circle

SAY • **In Jesus' name, Peter healed a man.** Peter explained that the man was healed by the power of Jesus. The man went into the temple praising God! The religious leaders wanted Peter and John to stop telling about Jesus, but they could not stop telling everyone the good news of Jesus.

Point to the Bible story picture on the giant timeline or big story circle as you ask the following review questions:

1. Why did the man's friends carry him to the temple every day? (*He could not walk or work. He asked people for money.*)
2. What did the man think Peter and John were going to give him? (*money*)
3. What did Peter do for the man? (*healed him*)
4. Who gave Peter power to heal the man? (*the Holy Spirit*)
5. What did Peter tell the religious leaders when they told him to stop telling about Jesus? (*"We cannot keep quiet. We must tell what we have seen and heard."*)

Learn the big picture question

SAY • Can you answer our big picture question? ***What does the Holy Spirit do? The Holy Spirit helps Christians.*** After Jesus went back to heaven, the Holy Spirit gave Jesus' followers power to begin working. When we turn from our sin and follow Jesus, God gives us the Holy Spirit too.

• Big Picture Question Poster

Practice the key passage

Open your Bible to Philippians 2:13. Read the key passage aloud several times. Sing together the key passage song.

SAY • God has work for each of us to do. He says so in the Bible. God works in us to help us do the work He gives us. Our key passage tell us this.

• Key Passage Poster
• "Working in You" song

Transition to experience the story

Experience THE STORY

SESSION TITLE: Peter Healed a Beggar
BIBLE PASSAGE: Acts 3:1-10; 4:5-31
MAIN POINT: In Jesus' name, Peter healed a man.
KEY PASSAGE: Philippians 2:13
BIG PICTURE QUESTION: What does the Holy Spirit do? The Holy Spirit helps Christians.

Definitions:
- lame - being unable to walk
- alms - money, food, or other things given to people in need

Sing "Silver and Gold Have I None"

Lead preschoolers in singing "Silver and Gold Have I None." If you are unfamiliar with the tune, look it up online. Consider downloading an MP3 to play for the children to sing along with. Explain words preschoolers may not understand.

"Peter and John went to pray;
   they met a lame man on the way.
   He asked for alms and held out his palms,
   and this is what Peter did say:

'Silver and gold have I none,
   but what I have I give to you.
   In the name of Jesus Christ
   of Nazareth, rise up and walk!'

He went walking and jumping and praising God,
   walking and jumping and praising God.
   'In the name of Jesus Christ
   of Nazareth, rise up and walk!' "

SAY • After Jesus went back to heaven, the Holy Spirit gave Jesus' followers power to begin working. With the power of Jesus' name, Peter healed a man who could not walk. **In Jesus' name, Peter healed a man**, and the man went into the temple praising God.

Assemble a flip book

Print a "flip book" for each preschooler. Invite preschoolers to cut apart the images and stack them in order. Use a stapler to fasten the images together. Use decorative tape to cover the staples and form a spine. Show preschoolers how to flip the pages to make the man jump up. Invite preschoolers to use their books to retell the Bible story.

SAY • **In Jesus' name, Peter healed a man** who could not walk. The Holy Spirit gave Peter the power to heal the man. Peter told the religious leaders, "This man was healed by the power of Jesus." The religious leaders could not stop Jesus' followers from telling people the good news about Jesus.

• "Flip Book" printable
• scissors
• stapler
• staples
• decorative tape

Spell *Jesus* with blocks

Gather blocks in groups of five. Place a strip of masking tape on the side of each block, and write each letter of *JESUS* on individual blocks. Mix up the blocks.

Write *JESUS* on a sheet of paper. Write *JESUS* on another sheet of paper arranging the letters vertically. Post the signs by the blocks. Invite preschoolers to stack the blocks to spell *JESUS*.

SAY • Jesus' name is the most powerful name there is. **In Jesus' name, Peter healed a man** who could not walk. Then the man went into the temple with Peter and John, and he praised God. Everyone who saw the man was amazed. This was the man who could not walk, but now he could walk!

• blocks
• masking tape
• marker
• construction paper

Toss coins

- towel
- paper plates
- coins
- painters tape (optional)

Lay a towel on the floor. Lay paper plates on the towel so that the towel is almost completely covered. Invite preschoolers to take turns tossing a coin onto the paper-plate-covered towel. Make a tape line for older preschoolers to stand behind as they toss. When the coins run out, count how many coins are on each paper plate and how many are on the towel or floor. Play again as time allows.

SAY • The man in our Bible story asked Peter and John for help. He thought they would give him money, maybe like these coins. But Peter said, "I do not have silver or gold. In the name of Jesus, stand up and walk." **In Jesus' name, Peter healed a man.** The Holy Spirit gave Jesus' followers power to do His work.

Walk, jump, and praise

- painters tape

Use two lines of painter's tape to make a path across the room. Invite preschoolers to line up single file on one end of the path. Explain that when you say "walk," a preschooler should walk along the path between the two tape lines. When you say "jump," a preschooler should jump down the path. When you say, "praise," a preschooler should say, "Jesus is King!" as they walk along the path. Allow preschoolers move along the path one at a time doing the appropriate motion.

SAY • **In Jesus' name, Peter healed a man.** His feet were strong, and he could walk and jump. Then the man went into the temple with Peter and John, and he praised God. The Holy Spirit gave Peter power to heal the man. The religious leaders could not stop Jesus' followers from telling people the good news about Jesus, and many people believed.

Snack

Play the countdown video to signal the end of activities. Guide preschoolers to clean their areas. Take a restroom break and wash hands. Gather preschoolers for snack time. Thank God for the snack.

Serve round golden crackers for snack. Remark how the crackers resemble a coin. Remind preschoolers that the man thought Peter and John would give him money, but Peter gave the man something better. **In Jesus' name, Peter healed a man.** The man went into the temple with his healed legs and praised God.

- countdown video (optional)
- Allergy Alert download
- snack food
- paper cups and napkins

Transition

When a child finishes her snack, guide her to throw away any trash. She may select a book or puzzle to examine, play quietly with play dough or a favorite toy, or color the Bible story coloring page.

Offer the journal page and invite preschoolers to draw a picture of the man who could not walk before, now jumping and praising God. Remind preschoolers that Peter could heal the man because Peter had the Holy Spirit. Peter healed the man in Jesus' name.

SAY • God, You are powerful, and You give Your people power when You give them the Holy Spirit. Thank You for trusting us to share the good news about Jesus. Help us to do the work You have given us by the power of the Holy Spirit. Amen.

If parents are picking up their children at this time, tell them something that their child enjoyed doing or did well during the session. Distribute the preschool big picture cards for families.

- books
- puzzles
- play dough
- Journal Page printable, 1 per child
- Bible Story Coloring Page
- crayons
- *Big Picture Cards for Families: Babies, Toddlers, and Preschoolers*

Stephen's Address

BIBLE PASSAGE: Acts 6:8–7:60

MAIN POINT: Stephen told people about Jesus, even when he would be hurt for it.

KEY PASSAGE: Philippians 2:13

BIG PICTURE QUESTION: What does the Holy Spirit do? The Holy Spirit helps Christians.

INTRODUCE THE STORY (15–20 MINUTES) PAGE 34		TELL THE STORY (10–15 MINUTES) PAGE 36		EXPERIENCE THE STORY (20–25 MINUTES) PAGE 38

Leader BIBLE STUDY

Stephen was one of the seven men chosen to serve as leaders in the early church at Jerusalem. (See Acts 6:1-7.) God blessed Stephen and gave him power to do wonders and miracles like some of the apostles.

Some of the Jews accused Stephen of blasphemy and dragged him to the Sanhedrin, a group of Jewish leaders who acted as a legal council. Stephen addressed the group. He drew from the Jewish history, which the leaders in the Sanhedrin would have known well. But Stephen taught from the Old Testament things the Jewish leaders had likely never realized.

As Stephen preached, he showed how the Old Testament pointed to a coming Savior and how that Savior was Jesus. Stephen pointed out that the Jews' ancestors had rejected God's prophets. And they were just like their fathers; they rejected the Messiah, the Lord Jesus. Not only did they reject Jesus, they killed Him!

The Jewish leaders rushed at Stephen. Stephen looked into heaven. He saw God's glory, and Jesus was standing at God's right hand. The Jews forced Stephen out of the city, and they stoned him.

Remind preschoolers of Jesus' words in Matthew 10:22: "You will be hated by everyone because of My name. But the one who endures to the end will be delivered." Following Jesus will include difficulty and suffering. Jesus gives words of both warning and comfort: "Don't be afraid" (Matt. 10:26).

Stephen was killed because he was a Christian. Jesus told His followers that they would be persecuted—hated, hurt, or even killed—for loving Him. (Mark 13:9-13; John 16:2) Jesus also said that those who suffer for Him would be blessed. (Matthew 5:11) Stephen was not afraid to die because he saw Jesus waiting for him in heaven. We can face suffering in this life because we know great joy is waiting for us in heaven.

MINISTRY GRID
training made simple

Additional resources for each session are available at *gospelproject.com.* For free training and session-by-session help, visit *www.ministrygrid.com/web/thegospelproject.*

The BIBLE STORY

Stephen's Address

Acts 6:8–7:60

• **Tell the story in the round:** Stand in the middle of the children as you tell the Bible story. Move around at appropriate moments.

• **Use Old Testament Bible Story Pictures:** Print and cut apart the "Old Testament Stories" printable. Hold up the appropriate picture as you mention that person in the Bible story.

Stephen was a man who **loved Jesus and served the church. God** was good to Stephen and **gave him power to do great things. One day, some Jews told lies about Stephen.** They did not like Stephen, and they wanted him to get in trouble.

The high priest asked Stephen if the Jews were telling the truth. No, they were not. Stephen taught the Jewish leaders about Jesus. He started in the Old Testament with stories about Abraham and Isaac, Joseph, and Moses.

In those days, God was working out His plan to bring someone into the world who could save people from their sin. God chose to do great things through His people, the Israelites. He rescued them from slavery in Egypt. And even though the people did not obey God or love God like they should, God did not give up on them.

God worked through Joshua and King David and King Solomon. **Stephen taught the religious leaders new things. He said that Jesus is the Messiah, and the religious leaders were wrong to reject Him and kill Him on the cross.**

The religious leaders were so angry! They did not like what Stephen was saying. But Stephen looked up and said, "I see the heavens opened and Jesus is standing at God's right side." Suddenly, the people yelled and rushed toward Stephen. They made Stephen leave the city, and then they threw rocks at him until he died.

Christ Connection: People hurt Stephen because he followed Jesus. Jesus told His friends that people would hurt them for loving Him. (Mark 13:9-13; John 16:2) When people are mean to us because we love Jesus, we can be brave because people hurt Jesus too. Jesus died and came back to life, and one day we will live with Him forever.

WANT TO DISCOVER GOD'S WORD? GET *MORE!*

Invite preschoolers to check out this week's devotionals to discover how God's Word can help them grow in the gospel. Order in bulk, subscribe quarterly, or purchase individually. For more information, check out *www.lifeway.com/ devotionals.*

Introduce THE STORY

SESSION TITLE: Stephen's Address

BIBLE PASSAGE: Acts 6:8–7:60

MAIN POINT: Stephen told people about Jesus, even when he would be hurt for it.

KEY PASSAGE: Philippians 2:13

BIG PICTURE QUESTION: What does the Holy Spirit do? The Holy Spirit helps Christians.

Welcome time

- "The Story" song
- offering basket
- Allergy Alert download
- favorite toys related to the Bible story theme

Play the unit theme song in the background as you greet preschoolers and follow your church's security procedures. Set an offering basket near the door to collect at an appropriate time. Post an allergy alert, if necessary. Set out a few favorite theme-related toys, such as puzzles and blocks.

Activity page

- "Dot-to-Dot" activity page, 1 per child
- pencils or crayons

Invite preschoolers to complete the dot-to-dot to reveal Jesus.

SAY • A man named Stephen saw a scene like this in today's Bible story. Listen to hear how much Stephen loved Jesus and how the Holy Spirit helped him.

Decide "Is it brave?"

Define *brave* for preschoolers as "being willing to do scary or hard things." Explain that you will call out an action. If preschoolers think a person must be brave to complete the action, they should stand up. If preschoolers do not think a person must to be brave to complete the action, they should sit down. Use the following statements or create your own.

- Petting a dog
- Climbing the monkey bars
- Trying a new food
- Inviting a new person to play with you
- Getting a shot at the doctor's office
- Sleeping without a night light
- Riding a bike with no training wheels
- Saying "no" to someone who wants you to do something wrong
- Telling someone about Jesus knowing he or she might hurt you

SAY • In today's Bible story, a man named **Stephen told people about Jesus, even when he would be hurt for it.** The Holy Spirit made Stephen brave. Listen to discover what happened to Stephen.

Invite a soldier to class

Invite a church member who has served in the armed forces to your class. Ask the guest to dress in his or her uniform if possible. Encourage him to share what life is like for a soldier. Give time for preschoolers to ask questions.

SAY • Today's Bible story is about a man named Stephen. Stephen was not a soldier, but God gave him a job to do that was very hard and scary. Let's find out what Stephen did in today's Bible story.

• guest

Tip: Make sure the guest does not share graphic details that could scare preschoolers.

Transition to tell the story

To gain the attention of all the preschoolers to move them to Bible study, show the countdown video, flip off the lights, or clap a simple rhythm for the children to copy. Invite preschoolers to give you a high-five as you move to Bible study.

• countdown video (optional)

Tell THE STORY

SESSION TITLE: Stephen's Address
BIBLE PASSAGE: Acts 6:8–7:60
MAIN POINT: Stephen told people about Jesus, even when he would be hurt for it.
KEY PASSAGE: Philippians 2:13
BIG PICTURE QUESTION: What does the Holy Spirit do? The Holy Spirit helps Christians.

Introduce the Bible story

Invite preschoolers to cover their ears.

SAY • Sometimes when we do not want to hear something, we cover our ears. The religious leaders in today's Bible study covered their ears because they did not want to hear what Stephen had to say, even though it was true.

Watch or tell the Bible story

- Bible
- bookmark
- "Stephen's Address" video
- Bible Story Picture Poster

Place a bookmark at Acts 6 in your Bible. Invite a preschooler to open it. Reverently display the open Bible.

SAY • The Bible is a true book. The stories we hear in the Bible really happened. God gives us His words in the Bible. Today's story is in the New Testament in Acts.

Show the video or tell the Bible story using the provided storytelling helps. Use the bolded version of the Bible story for young preschoolers.

Talk about the Bible story

- Main Point Poster
- Giant Timeline or Big Story Circle

SAY • **Stephen told people about Jesus, even when he would be hurt for it.** People lied about Stephen to get him in trouble. Stephen knew the Jewish leaders would not like hearing the truth about Jesus, but he told them anyway. Telling the good news is more important than anything else.

Point to the Bible story picture on the giant timeline or big story circle as you ask the following review questions:

1. Who gave Stephen power to do great things? (*God*)
2. What part of the Bible did Stephen use to teach the Jewish leaders, the Old Testament or the New Testament? (*Old Testament*)
3. What did Stephen say about Jesus? (*He is the Messiah. The religious leaders killed Him on a cross.*)
4. Did the religious leaders like what Stephen was saying? (*no*)
5. Whom did Stephen see standing at God's right side? (*Jesus*)

Learn the big picture question

SAY • Our big picture question is, ***What does the Holy Spirit do? The Holy Spirit helps Christians.*** Jesus told His friends that people would hurt them for loving Him. When people are mean to us because we love Jesus, we can ask the Holy Spirit to help us.

• Big Picture Question Poster

Practice the key passage

Open your Bible to Philippians 2:13. Read the key passage aloud several times. Sing together the key passage song.

• Key Passage Poster
• "Working in You" song

SAY • Sometimes the work God gives us to do can be very hard, but we can know that God will help us. He never leaves us to do things on our own. He is always at work in us.

Transition to experience the story

Experience THE STORY

SESSION TITLE: Stephen's Address

BIBLE PASSAGE: Acts 6:8–7:60

MAIN POINT: Stephen told people about Jesus, even when he would be hurt for it.

KEY PASSAGE: Philippians 2:13

BIG PICTURE QUESTION: What does the Holy Spirit do? The Holy Spirit helps Christians.

Play a loud/quiet game

Explain to preschoolers that when you count to three and say "loud," they must be as loud as they can. When you count to three and say "quiet," they must be absolutely quiet. If weather permits, play this game outdoors.

SAY • **Stephen told people about Jesus, even when he would be hurt for it.** The religious leaders did not like what Stephen was saying. They shouted as loud as they could at him. People hurt Stephen because he followed Jesus. Jesus told His friends that people would hurt them for loving Him. When people are mean to us because we love Jesus, we can be brave because people hurt Jesus too. Jesus died and came back to life, and one day we will live with Him forever.

Play a memory game

• "Old Testament Stories" printable
• scissors

Print the "Old Testament Stories" printable on heavyweight paper. Print in color if possible. Cut apart and set the cards faceup on a table. Allow preschoolers to examine each picture while you read the information on each one. Turn over the cards. Invite preschoolers to take turns flipping over two cards at a time to find a match. Keep the cards faceup for younger preschoolers.

SAY • Stephen taught the religious leaders about Jesus, starting with stories from the Old Testament. The leaders did not like what Stephen had to say, but **Stephen told people about Jesus, even when he would be hurt for it.** When people are mean to us because we love Jesus, we can be brave because people hurt Jesus too. Jesus died and came back to life, and one day we will live with Him forever.

Move rocks

Gather medium-sized rocks in a bucket. The rocks should be able to fit in a ladle. Place the bucket of rocks on one side of the room and an empty bucket on the other side of the room. Form a line behind the bucket of rocks. Direct the first preschooler in line to use the ladle to lift a rock out of the bucket, carry it across the room, drop it in the empty bucket, and return the ladle to the next child in line.

• buckets, 2 or more
• ladle, 1 or more
• medium-sized rocks

Play until all the rocks have been moved. Play again as time allows. For older preschoolers, form teams and use another ladle and set of buckets to compete to see who can move all their rocks to their empty bucket first.

SAY • People hurt Stephen for telling the truth about Jesus. **Stephen told people about Jesus, even when he would be hurt for it.** Following Jesus can be hard, but we can be brave because Jesus died and came back to life. No matter what happens, we know one day we will live with Him forever.

Play out teaching Bible stories

Set out Bibles, books, clipboards, small chalkboards, and chalk. Invite preschoolers to play out teaching Bible stories.

• Bibles
• books
• clipboards
• small chalkboards
• chalk

Guide preschoolers to take turns being the teacher.

SAY • Stephen taught the religious leaders new things. **Stephen told people about Jesus, even when he would be hurt for it.** He said that Jesus is the Messiah, and the religious leaders were wrong to reject Him and kill Him on the cross. Jesus died and came back to life, and one day we will live with Him forever.

Make prayer reminders

• empty tin cans,
  1 per child
• construction paper
• scissors
• tape
• markers
• stickers
• craft sticks, 5 per child
• duct tape (optional)
• map or globe

Suggested countries:
• North Korea
• Somalia
• Afghanistan
• Pakistan
• Sudan
• Syria
• Iraq
• Iran
• Yemen
• Eritrea

Before the session, cut construction paper strips to fit around a tin can. Write the main point on each strip. Give each preschooler a strip to decorate. Help her wrap the strip around an empty tin can and tape it in place. Use duct tape to cover any rough edges on the can.

Look online to find a list of countries where Christians are persecuted or use the provided suggestions. Write the name of each country on a craft stick. Make a set for each preschooler. Show preschoolers each country on a map or globe as you place the stick with the country's name on it in their prayer cans. Encourage preschoolers to place the cans on the table at home where they eat meals. Suggest that family members draw a stick from the can and pray for a country at each meal.

SAY • **Stephen told people about Jesus, even when he would be hurt for it.** Many believers around the world are being hurt for following Jesus. Let's pray for believers in these countries. Let's pray that they will be brave to tell others about Jesus and will keep following Him even though it is hard. Let's ask the Holy Spirit to help them remember that one day they will live with Jesus forever.

Snack

Play the countdown video to signal the end of activities. Guide preschoolers to clean their areas. Take a restroom break and wash hands. Gather preschoolers for snack time. Thank God for the snack.

Serve a normal snack and an unfamiliar snack such as an exotic fruit or something from an ethnic market. As preschoolers eat, remind them that **Stephen told people about Jesus, even when he would be hurt for it.** The bravery Stephen had was different than the bravery it takes to eat something new. The Holy Spirit made Stephen brave and gave him power to do what was very hard. *What does the Holy Spirit do? The Holy Spirit helps Christians.*

* countdown video (optional)
* Allergy Alert download
* snack food
* paper cups and napkins

Transition

When a child finishes his snack, guide him to throw away any trash. He may select a book or puzzle to examine, play quietly with play dough or a favorite toy, or color the Bible story coloring page.

Offer the journal page and invite children to draw Jesus standing in the sky. Remark that Stephen saw Jesus standing at God's right side. Encourage preschoolers that when people are mean to us because we love Jesus, we can be brave because people hurt Jesus too. Pray for the children.

SAY • God, Jesus said people might be mean to us because we love Him. When we are afraid, help us remember how Jesus was hurt so He could rescue us from sin. Make us brave. Amen.

If parents are picking up their children at this time, tell them something that their child enjoyed doing or did well during the session. Distribute the preschool big picture cards for families.

* books
* puzzles
* play dough
* Journal Page printable, 1 per child
* Bible Story Coloring Page
* crayons
* *Big Picture Cards for Families: Babies, Toddlers, and Preschoolers*

The Ethiopian Official Believed

BIBLE PASSAGE: Acts 8:26-40
MAIN POINT: Philip told the Ethiopian man about Jesus.
KEY PASSAGE: Philippians 2:13
BIG PICTURE QUESTION: What does the Holy Spirit do? The Holy Spirit helps Christians.

INTRODUCE THE STORY (15–20 MINUTES) PAGE 46	TELL THE STORY (10–15 MINUTES) PAGE 48	EXPERIENCE THE STORY (20–25 MINUTES) PAGE 50

4

Leader BIBLE STUDY

The believers in the early church faced intense persecution. After Stephen was killed, Jesus' followers at the church in Jerusalem scattered; however, they did not stop talking about Jesus. They continued to share the good news. One man, Philip, took the gospel to Samaria. The crowds there listened and believed, and they had great joy.

In today's Bible story, Philip was instructed by an angel of the Lord to go to a certain road in the desert. Philip obeyed. The Spirit led Philip to a chariot, where an Ethiopian official was reading the Scriptures from the prophet Isaiah. The Ethiopian man did not understand what he was reading, so Philip explained it to him.

The man was reading from the prophet Isaiah: "He was led like a sheep to the slaughter … In His humiliation justice was denied Him. … For His life is taken from the earth" (Acts 8:32-33). The official wondered if Isaiah was speaking about himself or another person. Philip told the official that Isaiah's words weren't about Isaiah; they were about the Messiah—Jesus! The official believed in Jesus and was baptized.

Guide preschoolers to consider the role of the Holy Spirit in this interaction between Philip and the Ethiopian official. Who was responsible for Philip's going to the desert? Who helped Philip explain the Scriptures? Who changed the heart of the official so he would believe?

After his interaction with the Ethiopian official, Philip continued sharing the gospel in all the towns on his way to the town of Caesarea.

4

In our mission of making disciples, believers must be willing instruments to be used in the hands of the Lord. Philip didn't go into the desert today with a strategy for converting another man; the Holy Spirit led Philip, and he obeyed. As believers, we can be open to the guidance of the Holy Spirit and willing to follow His lead. He will go with us.

 **MINISTRY GRID**
training made simple

Additional resources for each session are available at *gospelproject.com*. For free training and session-by-session help, visit *www.ministrygrid.com/web/thegospelproject*.

The God Who Empowers

The BIBLE STORY

**Bible
Storytelling
Tips**

The Ethiopian Official Believed
Acts 8:26-40

• **Travel with Philip:**
Use a brown or yellow
sheet to represent a
desert road. Cut a large
cardboard box to look
like a chariot. Use a
blue sheet to represent
water. Place the items
around the room. Lead
preschoolers to travel
to each setting at the
appropriate time as you
tell the Bible story.

• **Pantomime action:**
Invite two male guests
to pantomime the
actions of the Bible story
as you tell it.

Philip was one of the men Jesus sent out to tell people about Him. One day, an angel told Philip to go to a desert road. So Philip went.

On the road, Philip saw a man from Ethiopia. The man was an important official **who worked for the queen of Ethiopia. He was riding in a chariot and reading the words of the prophet Isaiah.**

The Holy Spirit led Philip to go to the man. Philip ran up to him and **asked, "Do you understand what you are reading?"**

The man said, "I need someone to teach it to me." Then he invited Philip into his chariot.

Philip sat with **the man**, who **was reading these words from Isaiah: "He was led like a sheep to be killed, and just like a lamb is quiet when its wool is cut, He does not say anything. What happened to Him was not fair. His life was taken away."**

The man asked, "Was Isaiah talking about himself or someone else?"

Isaiah was talking about the Messiah, so Philip began to teach the man the good news about Jesus.

As they traveled down the road, **they came to some water. The man asked the chariot to stop He wanted to be baptized because he believed in Jesus. Philip baptized the man in the water and the man went home happy.**

Christ Connection: The man from Ethiopia knew what the Bible said, but he did not know that the prophets were speaking about Jesus. The Holy Spirit led Philip to help the man understand the good news about Jesus: Jesus died on the cross for our sin, and He is alive, just like the prophets said.

WANT TO DISCOVER GOD'S WORD? GET *MORE!*

Invite preschoolers to check out this week's devotionals to discover how God's Word can help them grow in the gospel. Order in bulk, subscribe quarterly, or purchase individually. For more information, check out *www.lifeway.com/devotionals.*

Introduce THE STORY

SESSION TITLE: The Ethiopian Official Believed
BIBLE PASSAGE: Acts 8:26-40
MAIN POINT: Philip told the Ethiopian man about Jesus.
KEY PASSAGE: Philippians 2:13
BIG PICTURE QUESTION: What does the Holy Spirit do? The Holy Spirit helps Christians.

Welcome time

- "The Story" song
- offering basket
- Allergy Alert download
- favorite toys related to the Bible story theme

Play the unit theme song in the background as you greet preschoolers and follow your church's security procedures. Set an offering basket near the door to collect at an appropriate time. Post an allergy alert, if necessary. Set out a few favorite theme-related toys, such as puzzles and blocks.

Activity page

- "Trace the Path" activity page, 1 per child
- pencils or crayons

Invite preschoolers use their finger, a crayon, or pencil to trace the path from Philip to the man in the chariot. Then trace the path from the man in the chariot to the water.

SAY • Philip was a man Jesus sent out to tell people about Him. In today's Bible story, the Holy Spirit led Philip on a path where he met a man who needed to hear the good news. Let's discover how the Holy Spirit led Philip in today's Bible story.

Pass the Bible

- Bible

Invite preschoolers to sit in a circle on the floor. Give one child a Bible. Explain that when the music is playing preschoolers should pass the Bible around the circle. When the music stops, whoever is holding the Bible gets to ask the big picture question and the rest of the group will answer.

SAY • *What does the Holy Spirit do? The Holy Spirit helps Christians.* The Holy Spirit did some amazing things in the Bible story we will hear today. The Holy Spirit led Philip to a man who was reading the Bible. Listen for how the Holy Spirit led Philip to share the good news with the man and how the Holy Spirit helped the man believe the good news.

Draw on sand bags

Fill a gallon-sized ziplock bag half full of sand. Put the sand-filled ziplock bag inside another ziplock bag. Secure the opening of the bag with duct tape. Invite preschoolers to make handprints and footprints, draw, or write in the sand.

• clean play sand
• gallon-sized ziplock bags
• duct tape

SAY • We can find sand in many places like in a sand box, on the beach, or in the desert. In today's Bible story, the Holy Spirit led Philip to a desert road. The road was probably very sandy. Listen to our Bible story to find out what the Holy Spirit did on that desert road.

Transition to tell the story

To gain the attention of all the preschoolers to move them to Bible study, show the countdown video, flip off the lights, or clap a simple rhythm for the children to copy. Direct preschoolers where to sit as they move to Bible study one at a time. For example: "Rachel, please sit by Keith." "Sam, please sit by Alyssa."

• countdown video (optional)

Tell THE STORY

SESSION TITLE: The Ethiopian Official Believed
BIBLE PASSAGE: Acts 8:26-40
MAIN POINT: Philip told the Ethiopian man about Jesus.
KEY PASSAGE: Philippians 2:13
BIG PICTURE QUESTION: What does the Holy Spirit do? The Holy Spirit helps Christians.

Introduce the Bible story

• Bible

Open a Bible and read Isaiah 53:7-8.

SAY • Do you know whom these words are written about? In our Bible story, a man was reading these words from the Bible. He did not know he was reading about Jesus. The Holy Spirit sent someone to tell him.

Watch or tell the Bible story

• Bible
• bookmark
• "The Ethiopian Official Believed" video
• Bible Story Picture Poster

Place a bookmark at Acts 8 in your Bible. Invite a child to open to Acts. Reverently display the open Bible.

SAY • Someone was reading the Bible in today's Bible story. The Bible is the best book a person can read because it is the only book with God's words in it. God's words are true. Today's Bible story is in the Book of Acts.

Show the video or tell the Bible story using the provided storytelling helps. Use the bolded version of the Bible story for young preschoolers.

Talk about the Bible story

• Main Point Poster
• Giant Timeline or Big Story Circle

SAY • How amazing! The Holy Spirit led Philip to a man who was already reading about Jesus! He just didn't know it. **Philip told the Ethiopian man about**

Jesus. The Holy Spirit helped the man believe the truth about Jesus. He became a follower of Jesus.

Point to the Bible story picture on the giant timeline or big story circle as you ask the following review questions:

1. Whom did Philip see on the desert road? (*a man who worked for the queen of Ethiopia*)
2. Who led Philip to go up to the man? (*the Holy Spirit*)
3. Who was the man reading about? (*the Messiah, Jesus*)
4. What did Philip teach the man? (*the good news about Jesus*)
5. What did the man do to show he believed the good news about Jesus? (*He was baptized.*)

Learn the big picture question

SAY • Our big picture question is, ***What does the Holy Spirit do? The Holy Spirit helps Christians.*** The man from Ethiopia knew what the Bible said, but he did not know that the prophets were speaking about Jesus. The Holy Spirit led Philip to help the man understand the good news about Jesus: Jesus died on the cross for our sin, and He is alive, just like the prophets said.

• Big Picture Question Poster

Practice the key passage

Open your Bible to Philippians 2:13. Read the key passage aloud several times. Sing together the key passage song.

• Key Passage Poster
• "Working in You" song

SAY • Our key passage reminds us that God has a good plan in everything He does. God planned for Philip to tell the Ethiopian man about Jesus. God has plans to use us to share the good news with others too.

Transition to experience the story

Experience THE STORY

SESSION TITLE: The Ethiopian Official Believed

BIBLE PASSAGE: Acts 8:26-40

MAIN POINT: Philip told the Ethiopian man about Jesus.

KEY PASSAGE: Philippians 2:13

BIG PICTURE QUESTION: What does the Holy Spirit do? The Holy Spirit helps Christians.

Make scrolls

• paper
• markers
• string
• scissors

Give each preschooler a sheet of paper. Invite her to "write" on the paper. You may also write the name *JESUS* for preschoolers to trace. Guide preschoolers to roll up their paper and secure it with a piece of string.

SAY • The man from Ethiopia read Isaiah's words about Jesus on a scroll. The man from Ethiopia knew what the Bible said, but he did not know that the prophets were speaking about Jesus. **Philip told the Ethiopian man about Jesus.** The Holy Spirit led Philip to help the man understand the good news about Jesus: Jesus died on the cross for our sin, and He is alive, just like the prophets said.

Work Bible puzzles

• "Bible Puzzles" printable
• scissors

Print the "Bible Puzzles" printable on heavyweight paper. Print in color if possible. Cut each image into four to six puzzle pieces. Invite preschoolers to assemble the puzzles to reveal different Bible covers.

SAY • All these puzzles show a picture of a Bible. Bibles may look very different on the outside, but they all have God's words on the inside. The man from Ethiopia knew what the Bible said, but he did not know that the prophets were speaking about Jesus. **Philip told the Ethiopian man about Jesus.** Jesus died on the cross for our sin, and He is alive, just like the prophets said.

Sort coffee beans

Show preschoolers where Ethiopia is on a map or globe. Set a bowl of whole coffee beans on a table with a muffin pan. Invite preschoolers to count and sort the beans into the muffin cups. Consider providing nonbreakable coffee mugs for preschoolers to sort the coffee beans into using spoons.

SAY • The coffee plant these coffee beans came from was first found in Ethiopia. The man in our Bible story was an important official who worked for the queen of Ethiopia. **Philip told the Ethiopian man about Jesus.** The Holy Spirit led Philip to help the man understand the good news about Jesus. Let's pray the Holy Spirit will help more people in Ethiopia and right here in our country believe the good news about Jesus.

- Allergy Alert download
- map or globe
- bowl
- whole coffee beans
- muffin pan
- nonbreakable coffee mugs (optional)
- plastic spoons (optional)

Note: Caffeine may be absorbed through the skin. If parents have concerns about coffee beans, children may sort cacao nibs.

Play out the Bible story

Cut off one side of a large cardboard box. Cut two circles from the cardboard piece you removed. Use a marker to draw a wheel hub and spokes on the circles. Attach the "wheels" to the sides of the box. Invite preschoolers to take turns acting out the Bible story. Select one child to be the Ethiopian official sitting in the chariot looking at a Bible. Allow another child to be Philip walking along the road and climbing into the chariot to explain the Bible.

SAY • The man from Ethiopia knew what the Bible said, but he did not know that the prophets were speaking

- large cardboard box
- scissors
- marker
- masking tape
- Bible
- Bible times clothes (optional)

about Jesus. The Holy Spirit led Philip to the man's chariot. **Philip told the Ethiopian man about Jesus.** Jesus died on the cross for our sin, and He is alive, just like the prophets said.

Make kinetic sand

- Allergy Alert download
- large plastic bin
- flour, 8 cups
- cornmeal, 8 cups
- cooking oil, 1 cup
- corn syrup, 1 cup
- cups
- transportation toys (optional)

In a large plastic bin, combine 8 cups of flour with 8 cups of cornmeal. Then mix in 1 cup of oil and 1 cup of corn syrup. Stir the mixture. Invite preschoolers to use their fingers to combine the ingredients more thoroughly. Add more oil if the mixture feels too dry. Invite preschoolers to play in the sand with their hands and cups. Consider adding transportation toys to serve as the Ethiopian man's chariot.

SAY • Deserts are sandy places. Philip obeyed when the angel told him to go to the desert road. Then the Holy Spirit led Philip to go to the Ethiopian man. **Philip told the Ethiopian man about Jesus.** The Holy Spirit led Philip to help the man understand the good news about Jesus: Jesus died on the cross for our sin, and He is alive, just like the prophets said.

Snack

Play the countdown video to signal the end of activities. Guide preschoolers to clean their areas. Take a restroom break and wash hands. Gather preschoolers for snack time. Thank God for the snack.

Serve flatbread for snack. Tell preschoolers that people in Ethiopia eat a spongy flatbread called *injera* (in JEH ruh). Remind preschoolers that **Philip told the Ethiopian man about Jesus.** The Holy Spirit led Philip to help the man understand the good news about Jesus. ***What does the Holy Spirit do? The Holy Spirit helps Christians.***

- countdown video (optional)
- Allergy Alert download
- snack food
- paper cups and napkins

Transition

When a child finishes her snack, guide her to throw away any trash. She may select a book or puzzle to examine, play quietly with play dough or a favorite toy, or color the Bible story coloring page.

Offer the journal page and invite preschoolers to draw themselves sharing the good news about Jesus with someone they know. Remind preschoolers that the Holy Spirit led Philip to help the man understand the good news about Jesus. Pray for the children.

- books
- puzzles
- play dough
- Journal Page printable, 1 per child
- Bible Story Coloring Page
- crayons
- *Big Picture Cards for Families: Babies, Toddlers, and Preschoolers*

SAY • God, thank You for the Holy Spirit. Thank You that the Holy Spirit will help us do the work You have for us. Help us to share the good news about Your Son: Jesus died on the cross for our sin, and He is alive, just like the prophets said. Amen.

If parents are picking up their children at this time, tell them something that their child enjoyed doing or did well during the session. Distribute the preschool big picture cards for families.

Peter Visited Cornelius

BIBLE PASSAGE: Acts 10

MAIN POINT: Peter learned the gospel is for all people.

KEY PASSAGE: Philippians 2:13

BIG PICTURE QUESTION: What does the Holy Spirit do? The Holy Spirit helps Christians.

INTRODUCE THE STORY (15–20 MINUTES) PAGE 58	**TELL THE STORY** (10–15 MINUTES) PAGE 60	**EXPERIENCE THE STORY** (20–25 MINUTES) PAGE 62

 → →

Leader BIBLE STUDY

The apostle Peter preached and taught boldly after Pentecost. Jesus had commanded His followers to take the gospel to the ends of the earth. Acts 10 shows us how God made clear to Peter that the gospel is for everyone—not only the Jews but also the Gentiles.

The story begins in Caesarea (sess uh REE uh), the capital city in the Roman province of Judea. Cornelius, a Roman centurion, lived in Caesarea. Like many of the people in Caesarea, Cornelius was a Gentile; however, he did not worship the Roman gods. Cornelius worshiped the one true God, and one day, God spoke to Cornelius in a vision. In the vision, an angel told Cornelius to send for Peter.

Now Peter was in Joppa (JAHP uh), about 30 miles south of Caesarea. As Cornelius's men approached the city, Peter had a vision too. He was on a rooftop when God showed him a sheet of animals and commanded him to eat. The problem was that some of the animals were considered "unclean" by Jewish food laws. Three times, God said to Peter, "What God has made clean, do not call impure."

Peter visited Cornelius and others who had gathered with him. Peter understood that God did not want a Jewish man to call anyone unclean just because he was a foreigner. (See Acts 10:28-29.) Peter preached the gospel to the Gentiles there, and they believed. The Holy Spirit filled them, and they were baptized.

The gospel is good news for everyone. As you teach preschoolers, emphasize that God showed Peter that just as there is no "clean" and "unclean" food, there are no "clean" and "unclean" people. God calls believers to tell everyone the good news about Jesus, no matter who they are or where they come from. Jesus is the Lord of all!

5

MINISTRY GRID
training made simple

Additional resources for each session are available at *gospelproject.com*. For free training and session-by-session help, visit *www.ministrygrid.com/web/thegospelproject*.

The God Who Empowers

The BIBLE STORY

**Bible
Storytelling
Tips**

Peter Visited Cornelius

Acts 10

• **Use props for
Peter's vision:** Fill a
sheet with stuffed and
plastic animals. Enlist
a leader to lower the
sheet and open it in
front of children at the
appropriate moment in
the Bible story.

• **Move locations:**
Designate one side of
the room as Cornelius's
house and the other as
the house where Peter
was in the city. Lead
preschoolers from side
to side as you tell the
Bible story.

Cornelius was a Roman soldier. He loved God, helped other people, and prayed to God. **One day, God sent an angel to Cornelius.** The angel said, "Cornelius, God heard you when you prayed."

The angel told Cornelius to send some men into the city to find Peter. When the angel left, **Cornelius sent two servants and one soldier to the city.**

In the city, Peter went up on the roof of a house **to pray. Then Peter saw a vision. A vision is like a dream, but Peter was awake. He saw a big sheet coming down from heaven. In the sheet were all kinds of animals, snakes and lizards, and birds. A voice said, "Get up, Peter. Eat!"**

But Peter didn't want to. He **thought the animals were unclean. A voice said, "God has made these clean." Peter saw the vision three times,** and he tried to understand what it meant.

Then the men Cornelius sent into the city found the house where Peter was staying. They told Peter to come to Cornelius's house. So the next day, Peter went with the men.

When Peter saw Cornelius, he told him that the good news about Jesus is for all people, not just Jews. "Everyone who believes in Jesus will have their sins forgiven," Peter said.

The people there believed. Cornelius, his family, and his friends were baptized; and Peter stayed with them for a few days.

Christ Connection: God used a vision to show Peter that the good news about Jesus is for everyone. God wants believers to tell everyone the good news about Jesus no matter who they are or what they do. Jesus is the Lord of all.

WANT TO DISCOVER GOD'S WORD? GET *MORE!*

Invite preschoolers to check out this week's devotionals to discover how God's Word can help them grow in the gospel. Order in bulk, subscribe quarterly, or purchase individually. For more information, check out *www.lifeway.com/ devotionals.*

Introduce THE STORY

SESSION TITLE: Peter Visited Cornelius

BIBLE PASSAGE: Acts 10

MAIN POINT: Peter learned the gospel is for all people.

KEY PASSAGE: Philippians 2:13

BIG PICTURE QUESTION: What does the Holy Spirit do? The Holy Spirit helps Christians.

Welcome time

- "The Story" song
- offering basket
- Allergy Alert download
- favorite toys related to the Bible story theme

Play the unit theme song in the background as you greet preschoolers and follow your church's security procedures. Set an offering basket near the door to collect at an appropriate time. Post an allergy alert, if necessary. Set out a few favorite theme-related toys, such as puzzles and blocks.

Activity page

- "Find the Match" activity page, 1 per child
- pencils or crayons

Guide preschoolers to identify and circle the two animals in each row that match.

SAY • Peter was praying on a roof in today's Bible story when Peter saw a vision. A vision is like a dream, but Peter was awake. He saw a sheet with all kinds of animals, snakes and lizards, and birds. We will discover what God showed Peter through that vision in our Bible story.

March like a soldier

- tape
- construction paper

Use tape to create a square or rectangle path on the floor. Place a different color sheet of construction paper at each corner. Play music while preschoolers march as you lead them around the path. When you reach a sheet of construction paper, call out a physical activity for preschoolers to complete such as hopping on one foot three times, four jumping jacks, two squats, or a push-up. March until the music ends. Start the music again and march in the opposite direction.

SAY • One of the men in our Bible story today was a Roman soldier named Cornelius. Even though he was not Jewish, Cornelius loved God. God sent an angel to Cornelius. Listen to our Bible story to hear what the angel said to Cornelius.

Go on an animal safari

Before the session, print the "Animal Safari" printable in color, if possible. Post the images throughout the room. Make some more challenging to find than others. Invite preschoolers to go on a "safari" and locate all the animal images around the room. Preschoolers may play out being each animal that they find.

• "Animal Safari" printable
• tape

SAY • In the Old Testament, God gave His people rules about animals. Some animals were called clean and other animals were called unclean. God's people were not supposed to eat the unclean animals. In today's Bible story, God taught Peter something about the animals, but more importantly, God taught Peter something about the gospel, or good news about Jesus.

Transition to tell the story

To gain the attention of all the preschoolers to move them to Bible study, show the countdown video, flip off the lights, or clap a simple rhythm for the children to copy. Invite preschoolers to move to Bible study while pretending to be their favorite animal.

• countdown video (optional)

Tell THE STORY

SESSION TITLE: Peter Visited Cornelius

BIBLE PASSAGE: Acts 10

MAIN POINT: Peter learned the gospel is for all people.

KEY PASSAGE: Philippians 2:13

BIG PICTURE QUESTION: What does the Holy Spirit do? The Holy Spirit helps Christians.

Introduce the Bible story

Suggested statements:
- I have a brother.
- I have brown hair.
- I like to watch TV.
- I like to swing at the playground.

Tell preschoolers to stand up if you say a statement that describes them. For the last statement, say, "I am a person."

SAY • [*All preschoolers should be standing.*] Did you know that the good news about Jesus is for all people? Peter thought the good news was just for a special few. Have a seat and listen to what God showed Peter in today's Bible story.

Watch or tell the Bible story

- Bible
- bookmark
- "Peter Visited Cornelius" video
- Bible Story Picture Poster

Place a bookmark at Acts 10 in your Bible. Invite a preschooler to open it. Reverently display the open Bible.

SAY • God talks to us in the Bible, and everything God says is true. The Bible is the most important of all books. Today's Bible story is in Acts in the New Testament.

Show the video or tell the Bible story using the provided storytelling helps. Use the bolded version of the Bible story for young preschoolers.

Talk about the Bible story

- Main Point Poster
- Giant Timeline or Big Story Circle

SAY • God gave Peter a vision to teach him something important. Peter thought the good news about Jesus was just for the Jews, but he was wrong. **Peter**

learned the gospel is for all people. Everyone who believes in Jesus will have their sins forgiven.

Point to the Bible story picture on the giant timeline or big story circle as you ask the following review questions:

1. What did Peter see in the vision God gave him? (*all kinds of animals*)
2. What did a voice say when Peter did not want to eat the animals? (*"God has made these clean."*)
3. How many times did Peter see the vision? (*three*)
4. What did Peter's vision mean? (*The good news about Jesus is for all people.*)
5. Did Cornelius, his family, and his friends believe the truth about Jesus? (*yes*)

Learn the big picture question

SAY • Our big picture question asks, ***What does the Holy Spirit do? The Holy Spirit helps Christians.*** The Holy Spirit helps us do God's work. Part of the work God gives us is to tell everyone the good news about Jesus. The Holy Spirit helps us tell all people no matter who they are or what they do.

• Big Picture Question Poster

Practice the key passage

Open your Bible to Philippians 2:13. Read the key passage aloud several times. Sing together the key passage song.

SAY • God has a good plan that He is working out in the world and in each one of us. When we put our trust in Jesus, God works in us to complete His plan for us. He also uses us in His plan for the world too. He is a good God!

• Key Passage Poster
• "Working in You" song

Transition to experience the story

Experience THE STORY

SESSION TITLE: Peter Visited Cornelius

BIBLE PASSAGE: Acts 10

MAIN POINT: Peter learned the gospel is for all people.

KEY PASSAGE: Philippians 2:13

BIG PICTURE QUESTION: What does the Holy Spirit do? The Holy Spirit helps Christians.

Make a video telling the good news

LOW PREP

• mobile device

Tip: Follow your church's security procedures regarding videoing children.

Use a mobile device with a video application to make a video of each preschooler sharing the good news. Preschoolers may say the main point or "Everyone who believes in Jesus will have his or her sins forgiven." Consider sending a video of each child to his or her parents. Parents may post their child's video on social media to tell the good news.

SAY • Making a video is a fun way to tell the good news about Jesus to others. We can tell the good news about Jesus in many ways like in a letter, on the phone, or in person. The most important thing is that we tell it. **Peter learned the gospel is for all people.** God wants believers to tell everyone the good news about Jesus no matter who they are or what they do.

Build a town with blocks

• blocks
• people figures

Set out blocks and people figures. Invite preschoolers to build a city or town. Encourage them to use the people figures to play out telling the good news about Jesus.

SAY • How kind of God to send Peter to Cornelius's town! Cornelius, his family, and his friends all believed the good news about Jesus. **Peter learned the gospel is for all people.** God wants believers to share the gospel with everyone no matter who they are or what they do. Jesus is the Lord of all.

Make a mobile

Give each preschooler four different colors of multicultural people cutouts. Guide preschoolers to use markers or crayons to decorate their cutouts. Tie a length of yarn to each decorated cutout by punching a hole through the top.

Write *The gospel is for all people* on a paper towel tube for each preschooler. Invite preschoolers to use stickers to decorate the tube. Hang each people cutout from the paper towel tube by tying the yarn around the tube. (Older preschoolers who can tie knots may do this. Assist as needed.) Then run yarn through the length of the paper towel tube. Tie the ends together to form a hanging string.

SAY • Everyone who believes in Jesus will have their sins forgiven. **Peter learned the gospel is for all people.** God used a vision to show Peter that the good news about Jesus is for everyone. God wants believers to tell everyone the good news about Jesus no matter who they are or what they do. Jesus is the Lord of all.

- multicultural people die cuts
- markers or crayons
- blunt-tipped scissors
- yarn
- hole punch
- paper towel tubes
- stickers

Sort animals

Set out a variety of animals for preschoolers to sort. Preschoolers may sort animals based on where they live, how many legs they have, or by color. For older preschoolers, consider using Leviticus 11:2-47 or finding a list online to guide preschoolers in sorting the animals as clean and unclean.

SAY • Peter saw in a vision all kinds of animals, snakes and

- plastic animals
- bins

The God Who Empowers

lizards, and birds. God used the vision to show Peter that the good news about Jesus is for everyone. **Peter learned the gospel is for all people.** God wants believers to tell everyone the good news about Jesus no matter who they are or what they do. Jesus is the Lord of all.

Play with a sheet or parachute

- large sheet or parachute
- stuffed animals

Direct preschoolers to surround a large sheet or parachute and hold the edges. Place a stuffed animal in the middle of the sheet and invite preschoolers to make it pop up in the air. For a challenge, guide preschoolers to try to bounce the animal off the sheet between two certain preschoolers.

SAY • In his vision, Peter saw a big sheet coming down from heaven with animals in it. God used the vision to show Peter that the good news about Jesus is for everyone. **Peter learned the gospel is for all people.** God wants believers to tell everyone the good news about Jesus no matter who they are or what they do. Jesus is the Lord of all.

Snack

Play the countdown video to signal the end of activities. Guide preschoolers to clean their areas. Take a restroom break and wash hands. Gather preschoolers for snack time. Thank God for the snack.

Serve animal crackers for snack. Talk about how God gave Peter a vision where he saw all kinds of animals. God used the vision to show Peter that the good news about Jesus is for everyone. **Peter learned the gospel is for all people.** God wants believers to tell everyone the good news about Jesus no matter who they are or what they do.

Transition

When a child finishes his snack, guide him to throw away any trash. He may select a book or puzzle to examine, play quietly with play dough or a favorite toy, or color the Bible story coloring page.

Offer the journal page and invite preschoolers to draw people. Remind preschoolers that **Peter learned the gospel is for all people.** The good news about Jesus is for everyone. Jesus is the Lord of all. Pray for the children.

SAY • God, thank You that the good news about Jesus is not just for a few special people. The good news is for everyone, no matter who they are or what they do! Thank You for people who tell us the good news. Help us tell others the good news of how Jesus died on the cross and rose again to save people from sin. Amen.

If parents are picking up their children at this time, tell them something that their child enjoyed doing or did well during the session. Distribute the preschool big picture cards for families.

- countdown video (optional)
- Allergy Alert download
- snack food
- paper cups and napkins

- books
- puzzles
- play dough
- Journal Page printable, 1 per child
- Bible Story Coloring Page
- crayons
- Big Picture Cards for Families: Babies, Toddlers, and Preschoolers

Unit 29: Christmas

Unit Description:

God sent His Son, Jesus, to earth to be born as a baby in humble surroundings. Jesus was no ordinary baby. He was the One who would save God's people from their sin. Christmas is the time to celebrate God's greatest gift of Jesus Christ.

Key Passage:

1 John 4:9

Big Picture Question:

Why was Jesus born? Jesus was born to rescue us.

Unit 29: Christmas

Session 1:
Bible Story:
Angels Spoke to Mary and
Joseph
Bible Passage:
Matthew 1:18-24; Luke 1:26-56
Main Point:
God chose a family for Jesus.

Session 2:
Bible Story:
Jesus Was Born
Bible Passage:
Luke 2:1-20
Main Point:
Jesus was born as God
promised.

Angels Spoke to Mary and Joseph

BIBLE PASSAGE: Matthew 1:18-24; Luke 1:26-56
MAIN POINT: God chose a family for Jesus.
KEY PASSAGE: 1 John 4:9
BIG PICTURE QUESTION: Why was Jesus born? Jesus was born to rescue us.

INTRODUCE THE STORY
(15–20 MINUTES)
PAGE 72

TELL THE STORY
(10–15 MINUTES)
PAGE 74

EXPERIENCE THE STORY
(20–25 MINUTES)
PAGE 76

 → →

Leader BIBLE STUDY

People had been waiting a long time for Jesus. God hinted at His coming in the garden of Eden when He promised a seed to conquer the serpent. (Gen. 3:15) The prophets told of His coming hundreds of years before His birth. God was working out His plan to bring His people back to Himself.

In the Bible, God sometimes used angels to communicate His message to people. Angels spoke to Abraham in Genesis 18. The Angel of the Lord spoke to Balaam in Numbers 22. Now Mary and Joseph, the earthly parents of Jesus, each received a special visit from an angel to announce the birth of God's promised Messiah.

The angel Gabriel's announcement to Mary surprised her. By His grace, God chose Mary to be the mother of Jesus. The angel's message revealed much about this promised child.

First, He would be great in both being and nature. He would be the Son of the Most High. Jesus is the Son of God, and the Lord God promised to give Him the throne of His father David. These words fulfilled the prophecy given to David in 2 Samuel 7:12-16. He would reign over the house of Jacob forever. His kingdom would have no end.

The good news that Jesus was coming into the world was good news because of why He was coming. An angel revealed Jesus' purpose to Joseph in Matthew 1:21, "He will save His people from their sins." The gospel is the good news of what God has done for us through Christ.

The announcement of Jesus' birth is not the beginning of the gospel; God had been planning for this moment since before the beginning of time. (See Eph. 1:3-10.) Help the preschoolers you teach understand that God's plan has always been to save sinners and bring them back to Himself. Jesus, whose name means "Yahweh saves," is the culmination of that plan.

MINISTRY GRID
training made simple

Additional resources for each session are available at *gospelproject.com*. For free training and session-by-session help, visit *www.ministrygrid.com/web/thegospelproject*.

The BIBLE STORY

Bible Storytelling Tips

• **Use props:** Make paper bag or craft stick puppets for each person in the story: Mary, Joseph, Elizabeth, and the angel(s). Ask four or five adults to act out the story as the storyteller narrates it.

• **Move with the story:** Invite four or five adult helpers to dress up in Bible times clothes to play out the story. Encourage the adults to move around the room and use each corner as a different scene: Mary's house, Elizabeth's house, and Joseph's house.

Angels Spoke to Mary and Joseph

Matthew 1:18-24; Luke 1:26-56

One day, God sent an angel named Gabriel to a town called Nazareth. The angel went **to visit a young woman named Mary. Mary was engaged to be married to a man named Joseph.**

The angel said to Mary, "Be happy! God is happy with you. He is with you." Mary was afraid and did not understand. Why would God be happy with her? She hadn't done anything special.

"Do not be afraid," **the angel** said. He **told Mary that she was going to have a very special baby. The baby's name would be Jesus.**

Mary asked the angel, "How can that happen?"

The angel said, "God will be the Father of the baby. **The baby will be God's Son.**"

Then the angel said, "God can do anything!" **He told Mary that her relative Elizabeth was pregnant, even though she was old and did not have any children.**

"May everything happen just as you said," Mary said. Then the angel left.

Mary hurried to Elizabeth's house. When she arrived, the baby inside Elizabeth leaped for joy! The Holy Spirit filled **Elizabeth** and she **said, "What an honor, Mary! You and your baby will be blessed!"**

Mary was so happy. She **praised God with a song about how great God is.** Mary knew families in the future would say she was blessed because God was going to do great things through Jesus. God would keep His promise to Abraham to bless the whole world through his family by sending Jesus. Mary stayed with Elizabeth for three months.

Then she went home.

Joseph found out Mary was going to have a baby, but Joseph knew it was not his baby; Mary and Joseph were not married yet! Soon after Joseph thought these things, **an angel appeared to him in a dream.**

"**Joseph!**" the angel said. "**Do not be afraid to take Mary as your wife. Mary is going to have a son. Name Him Jesus because He is going to save His people from their sins!**"

When **Joseph** woke up, he did just what the angel said. He **married Mary, and when she had a son, Joseph named Him Jesus.**

Christ Connection: Many of God's prophets talked about Jesus before He was born. Everything they said about Jesus came true. Before God created the world, He planned to send Jesus. Jesus came to do God's plan, to rescue people from sin.

WANT TO DISCOVER GOD'S WORD? GET *MORE!*

Invite preschoolers to check out this week's devotionals to discover how God's Word can help them grow in the gospel. Order in bulk, subscribe quarterly, or purchase individually. For more information, check out *www.lifeway.com/devotionals.*

Introduce THE STORY

SESSION TITLE: Angels Spoke to Mary and Joseph
BIBLE PASSAGE: Matthew 1:18-24; Luke 1:26-56
MAIN POINT: God chose a family for Jesus.
KEY PASSAGE: 1 John 4:9
BIG PICTURE QUESTION: Why was Jesus born? Jesus was born to rescue us.

Welcome time

- "O Come" song
- offering basket
- Allergy Alert download
- favorite toys related to the Bible story theme

Play the unit theme song in the background as you greet preschoolers and follow your church's security procedures. Set an offering basket near the door to collect at an appropriate time. Post an allergy alert, if necessary. Set out a few favorite theme-related toys, such as puzzles and blocks.

Activity page

- "Find the Parents" activity page, 1 per child
- pencils or crayons

Invite preschoolers to look at the baby on the left and circle the parents on the right.

SAY • Good job choosing the parents! Did you know that Jesus had parents too? God is Jesus' Father, but Jesus' parents on earth were Mary and Joseph. In today's Bible story, we will hear how God told Mary and Joseph that they would be Jesus' parents.

Draw family pictures

Set out paper and encourage preschoolers to draw a picture of their families. Ask preschoolers about their family members as they work.

SAY • God chose you to be part of your family. Did you know that Jesus had a family? In today's Bible story, we will hear how **God chose a family for Jesus.** Jesus is God's Son, but God chose Mary to be Jesus' mother and Joseph to be Jesus' earthly father.

• paper
• markers or crayons

Sort Christmas gift bows

Gather an assortment of Christmas bows. Invite preschoolers to sort the bows into gift boxes. If the bows are adhesive, consider allowing preschoolers to place the bows on gift boxes.

SAY • We put Christmas bows on Christmas gifts. At Christmastime, we celebrate the greatest gift we have ever received—Jesus! Christmas is the time of the year the church remembers how Jesus came from heaven to earth as a baby. Listen to today's Bible story to hear whom God chose to be Jesus' parents on earth.

• Christmas gift bows
• gift boxes

Transition to tell the story

To gain the attention of all the preschoolers to move them to Bible study, show the countdown video, flip off the lights, or clap a simple rhythm for the children to copy. Invite preschoolers to make their happiest face as they move to Bible study.

• countdown video (optional)

Tell THE STORY

SESSION TITLE: Angels Spoke to Mary and Joseph
BIBLE PASSAGE: Matthew 1:18-24; Luke 1:26-56
MAIN POINT: God chose a family for Jesus.
KEY PASSAGE: 1 John 4:9
BIG PICTURE QUESTION: Why was Jesus born? Jesus was born to rescue us.

Introduce the Bible story

• baby picture

Show a picture of you as a baby or your children as babies.
SAY • Jesus was in heaven with God, but He came to earth as a baby. Why would Jesus do that? Listen to our Bible story to find out.

Watch or tell the Bible story

• Bible
• bookmark
• "Angels Spoke to Mary and Joseph" video
• Bible Story Picture Poster

Place a bookmark at Matthew or Luke in your Bible. Invite a preschooler to open it. Reverently display the open Bible.
SAY • Is there any book more important than the Bible? No, the Bible has God's words in it. The stories in the Bible really happened. Today's Bible story comes from two books in the New Testament: Matthew and Luke.
Show the video or tell the Bible story using the provided storytelling helps. Use the bolded version of the Bible story for young preschoolers.

Talk about the Bible story

• Main Point Poster
• Giant Timeline or Big Story Circle

SAY • God planned for Mary and Joseph to have an important part of His plan to rescue the world from sin. **God chose a family for Jesus.** God chose Mary and Joseph to be Jesus' earthly parents. By sending Jesus, God would keep His promise to bless the

Preschool Leader Guide
Unit 29 • Session 1

whole world through Abraham's family.

Point to the Bible story picture on the giant timeline or big story circle as you ask the following review questions:

1. What did the angel say was going to happen to Mary? (*She was going to have a very special baby named Jesus.*)
2. Whom did Mary go see after the angel told her the special news? (*her relative Elizabeth*)
3. What part did Mary and Joseph have in God's plan? (*to be Jesus' parents on earth*)
4. What did Jesus come into the world to do? (*to save people from their sins*)

Learn the big picture question

SAY • Many of God's prophets talked about Jesus before He was born. Everything they said about Jesus came true. Our big picture question asks, ***Why was Jesus born? Jesus was born to rescue us.*** Before God created the world, He planned to send Jesus. Jesus came to do God's plan, to rescue people from sin.

• Big Picture Question Poster

Practice the key passage

Open your Bible to 1 John 4:9. Read the key passage aloud several times. Sing together the key passage song.

SAY • God knew we would sin and need a Savior. All along God planned to send His one and only Son into the world to be punished for sin. Because Jesus came into the world, we can be saved.

• Key Passage Poster
• "One and Only Son" song

Transition to experience the story

Experience THE STORY

SESSION TITLE: Angels Spoke to Mary and Joseph
BIBLE PASSAGE: Luke 1:26-56; Matthew 1:18-24
MAIN POINT: God chose a family for Jesus.
KEY PASSAGE: 1 John 4:9
BIG PICTURE QUESTION: Why was Jesus born? Jesus was born to rescue us.

Sing Christmas carols

• "O Come" song (optional)
• "One and Only Son" song (optional)

Lead preschoolers in singing familiar Christmas carols that relate to the birth of Jesus. Suggestions include "Joy to the World," "Away in a Manger," "Silent Night," "Hark the Herald Angels Sing," "O Come All Ye Faithful," and "Go, Tell It on the Mountain." You may also play the key passage or theme song.

SAY • We sing songs at Christmas that remind us of what God did for us when He sent Jesus. In our Bible story, Mary praised God with a song about how great God is. **God chose a family for Jesus.** Before God created the world, He planned to send Jesus. Jesus came to do God's plan, to rescue people from sin.

Taste baby food

• Allergy Alert download
• baby food (single fruit or vegetable serving)
• plastic spoons
• foam plates (optional)

Bring a variety of baby foods. Open each one. Place some baby food on a plastic spoon for a preschooler to sample. Be careful that each spoon is only used one time. Make the tasting a game by removing labels and inviting preschoolers to guess each food.

SAY • What kind of food do you think Baby Jesus ate? Do you think Mary and Joseph mashed up His food so He could eat it? **God chose a family for Jesus.** Many of God's prophets talked about this Baby long before He was born. Everything they said about Jesus came true.

Stamp Christmas cards

Squirt various colors of washable paint onto individual foam plates. Set out cookie cutters. Give each preschooler a sheet of white construction paper. Guide a child to fold his sheet in half to form a card. Demonstrate how to press a cookie cutter in the paint and then stamp the paper. Invite preschoolers to stamp images on their Christmas cards.

- white construction paper
- angel, candy cane, or sheep cookie cutters
- washable paint
- foam plates
- wipes for cleanup
- smocks

SAY • We give Christmas cards at Christmastime to celebrate that God sent His Son to earth. Many of God's prophets talked about Jesus before He was born. Everything they said about Jesus came true. **God chose a family for Jesus.** Jesus came to do God's plan, to rescue people from sin.

Examine evergreens

Set out a variety of Christmas greenery for preschoolers to examine. Suggestions include pine, cedar, magnolia, fir, holly (with thorns clipped), ivy, boxwood, eucalyptus, balsam, and juniper. Encourage preschoolers to feel and smell the nature items. Provide magnifying glasses for preschoolers to examine the greenery closely.

- Allergy Alert download
- evergreens (real or artificial)
- magnifying glasses

Tip: Make sure preschoolers do not put evergreens in their mouths.

SAY • These plants are called *evergreens*. That is because they stay green all the time. Their leaves do not die. Evergreens remind us of Jesus. Jesus died on the cross, but God raised Him from the dead to live forever. When we put our trust in Jesus, we will have life forever with God. *Why was Jesus born? Jesus was born to rescue us.*

Visit with a baby

• guests
• hand sanitizer

Note: Instruct preschoolers who want to touch the baby (with parents' permission) to rub the baby's feet.

Invite a few parents to visit your class with their babies. Vary the ages of the babies. Include newborns as well as toddlers. (Most preschoolers consider children younger than themselves to be babies!) Encourage preschoolers to make friendly faces at the babies and play with them as the parents allow.

SAY • Can you imagine Jesus being a baby like one of these? Do you think Baby Jesus giggled and cried? Do you think Mary and Joseph smiled at Baby Jesus or played peekaboo with Him? **God chose a family for Jesus.** Jesus came to do God's plan to rescue people from sin.

Snack

Play the countdown video to signal the end of activities. Guide preschoolers to clean their areas. Take a restroom break and wash hands. Gather preschoolers for snack time. Thank God for the snack.

Serve O-shaped cereal for snack. Point out to preschoolers that babies often eat O-shaped cereal. Talk about how Jesus came to earth as a baby. *Why was Jesus born? Jesus was born to rescue us.* God knew we needed someone to save us from sin, so He sent His very own Son. Jesus came from heaven to earth. Jesus never sinned, so only He could take the punishment for our sin.

- countdown video (optional)
- Allergy Alert download
- snack food
- paper cups and napkins

Transition

When a child finishes his snack, guide him to throw away any trash. He may select a book or puzzle to examine, play quietly with play dough or a favorite toy, or color the Bible story coloring page.

Offer the journal page and invite preschoolers to draw a picture of Baby Jesus with Mary and Joseph. **God chose a family for Jesus.** God shared His plan with Mary and Joseph, and they obeyed. Pray for the children.

SAY • God, thank You that everything Your prophets wrote about Jesus came true. Thank You for keeping Your promise to send a Savior. Thank You that Jesus did Your plan to rescue us from sin. Help us to turn from our sin and follow Him. Amen.

If parents are picking up their children at this time, tell them something that their child enjoyed doing or did well during the session. Distribute the preschool big picture cards for families.

- books
- puzzles
- play dough
- Journal Page printable, 1 per child
- Bible Story Coloring Page
- crayons
- *Big Picture Cards for Families: Babies, Toddlers, and Preschoolers*

2

Jesus Was Born

BIBLE PASSAGE: Luke 2:1-20
MAIN POINT: Jesus was born as God promised.
KEY PASSAGE: 1 John 4:9
BIG PICTURE QUESTION: Why was Jesus born? Jesus was born to rescue us.

INTRODUCE THE STORY
(15–20 MINUTES)
PAGE 84

TELL THE STORY
(10–15 MINUTES)
PAGE 86

EXPERIENCE THE STORY
(20–25 MINUTES)
PAGE 88

 → →

Leader BIBLE STUDY

Do you think it was just by chance that Caesar Augustus called for a census? Did it just so happen that Mary and Joseph were traveling to Bethlehem—the very place the Messiah was prophesied to be born? (Micah 5:2) God is in control of all things, which He showed by using a pagan emperor to bring about His plan.

After Jesus was born, Mary laid Him in a manger. A king in a manger! It was so unlikely. But Jesus was no ordinary baby. He was God's Son, sent in the most humble of positions, "not to be served, but to serve, and to give His life—a ransom for many" (Matt. 20:28).

Imagine the shepherds' surprise when an angel of the Lord suddenly appeared. The Bible says that they were terrified! But the angel said to them, "Don't be afraid, for look, I proclaim to you good news of great joy that will be for all the people: Today a Savior, who is Messiah the Lord, was born for you in the city of David" (Luke 2:10-11).

What a relief! This angel had come to bring good news. First, he proclaimed a Savior. The people of Israel were well aware of their need for a Savior. They made sacrifices daily to atone for their sin. Finally, a Savior had come who would be the perfect sacrifice for sin, once and for all.

Jesus was also Messiah the Lord. The word *Messiah* means "Anointed One," especially a king. The Deliverer and Redeemer would be King over His people. And this was all happening in Bethlehem, the city of David—just as the prophet Micah said.

This is the best news ever! An army of angels appeared, praising God and saying: "Glory to God in the highest heaven, and peace on earth to people He favors" (Luke 2:14). The purpose of Jesus' birth was twofold: to bring glory to God and to make peace between God and those who trust in Jesus' death and resurrection.

MINISTRY GRID
training made simple

Additional resources for each session are available at *gospelproject.com*. For free training and session-by-session help, visit *www.ministrygrid.com/web/thegospelproject*.

The BIBLE STORY

Jesus Was Born
Luke 2:1-20

• **Use a manger scene:** Move and arrange the pieces of a manger scene at the appropriate moments as you tell the Bible story.

• **Act it out:** Place a baby doll in a box. Invite two preschoolers to play Mary and Joseph. Choose several preschoolers to play shepherds and stand on the other side of the room. Encourage another child to be the angel and the rest of the group to be the host of angels singing praises. Lead preschoolers to act out their roles at the appropriate moments in the Bible story.

When Mary was pregnant with Baby Jesus, a man named Caesar Augustus sent out an order to all the people in the land: "Everyone must go to his hometown to be counted!" Caesar Augustus was the emperor of Rome, and he wanted a list of all the people who were living in the land.

Since **Joseph** was part of King David's family, he **and Mary** left Nazareth and **traveled to Bethlehem**, the city of David.

While **they** were there, Mary was ready to have her baby. Mary and Joseph **looked for a safe place to stay, but every place was full** because of all the people who were in town to be counted. **So Mary and Joseph found a place where animals were kept, and that is where Mary had her baby, Jesus. She wrapped Him in cloth** so He would be snug and warm, **and** she **laid Him in a manger.**

Nearby, some shepherds were staying out in the fields and watching their sheep to protect them from thieves and wild animals. **All of a sudden, an angel of the Lord stood before them. A bright light shone around the shepherds, and they were scared!**

But the angel said to them, **"Do not be afraid! I have good news for you: Today a Savior, who is Messiah the Lord, was born for you** in the city of David." Then the angel said, **"Go find the baby. He will be wrapped in cloth and lying in a manger."**

All of a sudden, many angels appeared. They praised God and said, "Glory to God in the highest heaven, and peace on earth to people He favors!"

So **the shepherds went** straight to Bethlehem **to find Baby Jesus. They found Him, and they told others about Him. Everyone who heard about Jesus was surprised and amazed.** Mary thought about everything that was happening and tried to understand it. The shepherds returned to their fields, and they praised God because **everything had happened just as the angel had said.**

Christ Connection: Jesus was born! This was very good news! Jesus was not like other babies. Jesus is God's Son. God sent Jesus to earth from heaven. Jesus came into the world to save people from their sins and to be their King.

WANT TO DISCOVER GOD'S WORD? GET MORE!

Invite preschoolers to check out this week's devotionals to discover how God's Word can help them grow in the gospel. Order in bulk, subscribe quarterly, or purchase individually. For more information, check out *www.lifeway.com/ devotionals.*

Introduce THE STORY

SESSION TITLE: Jesus Was Born

BIBLE PASSAGE: Luke 2:1-20

MAIN POINT: Jesus was born as God promised.

KEY PASSAGE: 1 John 4:9

BIG PICTURE QUESTION: Why was Jesus born? Jesus was born to rescue us.

Welcome time

- "O Come" song
- offering basket
- Allergy Alert download
- favorite toys related to the Bible story theme

Play the unit theme song in the background as you greet preschoolers and follow your church's security procedures. Set an offering basket near the door to collect at an appropriate time. Post an allergy alert, if necessary. Set out a few favorite theme-related toys, such as puzzles and blocks.

Activity page

- "What Does Not Belong?" activity page, 1 per child
- pencils or crayons

Invite preschoolers to circle the things that do not belong in the picture.

SAY • What did you circle? Some of the things we see at Christmastime do not really have much to do with the reason we celebrate Christmas. Christmas is the time we celebrate when Jesus came to earth as a baby. There were no Christmas lights or wreaths. There were no decorations, even though Jesus' birth was the most important thing that had ever happened.

Count things

- classroom items
- counting manipulatives (optional)

Invite preschoolers to count various items throughout the room. Suggestions include markers, toys, puzzles, and so forth. You may also set out counting manipulatives you have on hand.

SAY • How many friends are in our class at church today? Will you help me count? [*Count the number of children in the class aloud.*] When Mary was pregnant with Baby Jesus, a man named Caesar Augustus sent out an order to all the people in the land: "Everyone must go to his hometown to be counted!" Caesar Augustus was the emperor of Rome, and he wanted a list of all the people who were living in the land. Listen to our story to discover where Jesus was born.

Pack for a journey

Provide a few suitcases or totes, clothes, and various items for preschoolers to pack. Set up the suitcases and items in one corner of the room and call that part of the room *Nazareth*. Designate another part of the room to be *Bethlehem*. Invite preschoolers to pack and travel to Bethlehem.

• suitcases or totes
• various items for children to pack

SAY • Long ago, God said through His prophet Micah that His Son would be born in Bethlehem. In our Bible story, we'll find out how God brought Mary and Joseph to Bethlehem at just the right time for Jesus to be born.

Transition to tell the story

To gain the attention of all the preschoolers to move them to Bible study, show the countdown video, flip off the lights, or clap a simple rhythm for the children to copy. Invite preschoolers to make barnyard animal sounds as they move to Bible study.

• countdown video (optional)

Tell THE STORY

SESSION TITLE: Jesus Was Born
BIBLE PASSAGE: Luke 2:1-20
MAIN POINT: Jesus was born as God promised.
KEY PASSAGE: 1 John 4:9
BIG PICTURE QUESTION: Why was Jesus born? Jesus was born to rescue us.

Introduce the Bible story

Ask children to tell what they love most about Christmas.

SAY • There are so many special things to see and do at Christmastime. But nothing is more special than God sending His very own Son to earth as a baby. Jesus is the reason we celebrate. Listen to our Bible story to hear how Jesus came to us.

Watch or tell the Bible story

• Bible
• bookmark
• "Jesus Was Born" video
• Bible Story Picture Poster

Place a bookmark at Luke 2 in your Bible. Invite a preschooler to open it. Reverently display the open Bible.

SAY • The Bible is God's Word. The stories we read about in the Bible are true because God always speaks the truth. God sent Jesus to earth! Today's Bible story comes from the New Testament Book of Luke.

Show the video or tell the Bible story using the provided storytelling helps. Use the bolded version of the Bible story for young preschoolers.

Talk about the Bible story

• Main Point Poster
• Giant Timeline or Big Story Circle

SAY • Many of God's prophets talked about Jesus before He was born. Everything they said about Jesus came true. **Jesus was born as God promised.** Before God created the world, He planned to send Jesus. Jesus was not like other babies. Jesus is God's Son. God sent Jesus to earth from heaven. Jesus came to save people from their sins and to be their King.

Point to the Bible story picture on the giant timeline or big story circle as you ask the following review questions:

1. To what city did Mary and Joseph travel? (*Bethlehem*)
2. Why did Mary and Joseph have to stay in a place where animals were kept? (*Every place was full.*)
3. How did the shepherds feel when the angel of the Lord stood before them? (*scared*)
4. Who told the shepherds where to find Jesus? (*an angel*)
5. What did the shepherds do after they found Baby Jesus? (*They told others about Him.*)

Learn the big picture question

SAY • Do you remember our big picture question and answer? ***Why was Jesus born? Jesus was born to rescue us.*** Jesus is God's Son. Jesus was in heaven with God, but He came to earth as a human baby so He could grow up to rescue us from sin.

• Big Picture Question Poster

Practice the key passage

Open your Bible to 1 John 4:9. Read the key passage aloud several times. Sing together the key passage song.

• Key Passage Poster
• "One and Only Son" song

SAY • Our key passage reminds us how much God loves people. He sent Jesus from heaven to our sinful world as a baby. Sending Jesus was the way God rescued us from sin. He loves us so much!

Transition to experience the story

Experience THE STORY

SESSION TITLE: Jesus Was Born
BIBLE PASSAGE: Luke 2:1-20
MAIN POINT: Jesus was born as God promised.
KEY PASSAGE: 1 John 4:9
BIG PICTURE QUESTION: Why was Jesus born? Jesus was born to rescue us.

- "O Come" song (optional)
- "One and Only Son" song (optional)

Play musical chairs

Set out one fewer chair than there are children. Arrange the chairs in a circle facing outward. Preschoolers should walk around the circle of chairs as Christmas music plays. When the music stops, preschoolers must find a chair to sit in. The child who does not find a chair gets to ask the big picture question and invite the rest of the group to respond.

SAY • There were not enough chairs for all of you to sit, just like there were not enough places to stay when Mary and Joseph arrived in Bethlehem. *Why was Jesus born? Jesus was born to rescue us.* God planned all along that Jesus would be born in a place where animals were kept. God sent Jesus to earth from heaven. Jesus came into the world to save people from their sins and to be their King.

- Allergy Alert download
- birthday party decorations
- birthday hats
- noisemakers
- cake or cupcakes
- paper plates
- napkins
- cups
- plastic forks

Host a "Happy Birthday, Jesus!" party

Decorate the room. Provide birthday hats and noisemakers. Lead preschoolers to sing the "Happy Birthday" song to Jesus. Invite children to blow the noisemakers and shout "hooray!" Serve birthday cake or cupcakes for snack to celebrate Jesus' birthday.

SAY • We celebrate Jesus' birthday at Christmas because His birthday is the most special birthday in all of history! Jesus is God's Son sent from heaven to earth! **Jesus was born as God promised.** This is good news! We want to thank God for sending Jesus to save people from sin.

Make Christmas puzzles

Gather Christmas cards depicting images of the Christmas story from the Bible. Cut apart the cards so only the picture remains. Provide a picture for each preschooler. Invite preschoolers to cut their pictures into four to six pieces to create a puzzle. Lead preschoolers to work one another's puzzles. Review the Bible story as preschoolers work. Store each puzzle in a ziplock bag to send home with preschoolers.

• Christmas cards depicting the Christmas story
• blunt-tipped scissors
• ziplock bags

SAY • Our puzzles remind us that **Jesus was born as God promised.** This was very good news! Jesus was not like other babies. Jesus is God's Son. God sent Jesus to earth from heaven. Jesus came into the world to save people from their sins and to be their King.

Care for babies

Set out baby dolls, blankets, bottles, and other items for preschoolers to play out caring for babies. Demonstrate how to swaddle the babies with a blanket. Explain to preschoolers that Mary and Joseph took care of Jesus when He was born.

• baby dolls
• blankets
• baby doll bottles (optional)

SAY • Mary wrapped Jesus in cloth so He would be snug and warm, and she laid Him in a manger. **Jesus was born as God promised.** This was very good news! Jesus was not like other babies. Jesus is God's Son. God sent Jesus to earth from heaven. Jesus came into the world to save people from their sins and to be their King.

Build a stable with blocks

- blocks
- baby doll
- blankets

Invite children to use blocks to build a stable. Encourage preschoolers to wrap a baby doll in a blanket and place it in the block stable.

SAY • Mary and Joseph looked for a safe place to stay, but every place was full because of all the people who were in town to be counted. So Mary and Joseph found a place where animals were kept, and that is where Mary had her baby Jesus. **Jesus was born as God promised.** Jesus came into the world to save people from their sins and to be their King.

Snack

Play the countdown video to signal the end of activities. Guide preschoolers to clean their areas. Take a restroom break and wash hands. Gather preschoolers for snack time. Thank God for the snack.

Serve animal crackers for today's snack. Invite preschoolers to hold up a sheep and say "baaa" if they find a sheep in their snack mix. Talk about how God sent angels to tell shepherds that His Son was born in Bethlehem. **Jesus was born as God promised.** When the shepherds found Baby Jesus, they told others about Him. The shepherds returned to their fields, and they praised God because everything had happened just as the angel had said.

- countdown video (optional)
- Allergy Alert download
- snack food
- paper cups and napkins

Transition

When a child finishes her snack, guide her to throw away any trash. She may select a book or puzzle to examine, play quietly with play dough or a favorite toy, or color the Bible story coloring page.

Offer the journal page and invite preschoolers to draw a picture of Baby Jesus in the manger. Remind preschoolers that Jesus was not born in a palace like a king, even though He is King over everything. Jesus came to rescue us from sin. Pray for the children.

SAY • God, thank You for sending Jesus to earth as a baby. Jesus came into the world to save us from our sin and to be our King. Help us to turn from sin and follow Him. Amen.

If parents are picking up their children at this time, tell them something that their child enjoyed doing or did well during the session. Distribute the preschool big picture cards for families.

- books
- puzzles
- play dough
- Journal Page printable, 1 per child
- Bible Story Coloring Page
- crayons
- Big Picture Cards for Families: Babies, Toddlers, and Preschoolers

Unit 30: The God Who Sends

Unit Description:

In time, Paul, who was one of the greatest missionaries of all time, took the gospel of Jesus Christ throughout the Roman empire, growing the church even more. God's promise to bless all the people of the earth was being fulfilled.

Key Passage:

Acts 1:8

Big Picture Question:

How do people hear about Jesus? God uses Christians to tell others about Jesus.

Unit 30: The God Who Sends

Session 1:
Bible Story:
Paul's Conversion and Baptism
Bible Passage:
Acts 9:1-25
Main Point:
Jesus saved Saul from his sins.

Session 2:
Bible Story:
Paul's First Journey
Bible Passage:
Acts 13:1-3; 14:8-28
Main Point:
The Holy Spirit sent Paul and Barnabas to tell people about Jesus.

Session 3:
Bible Story:
The Message: "Christ Alone"
Bible Passage:
Acts 15:1-35
Main Point:
The church encouraged Gentile believers.

Session 4:
Bible Story:
Paul's Second Journey
Bible Passage:
Acts 16:11-34
Main Point:
Paul and Silas told all kinds of people about Jesus.

Session 5:
Bible Story:
Paul Preached in Europe
Bible Passage:
Acts 17:16-34
Main Point:
Paul taught the people in Athens about the one true God.

Session 6:
Bible Story:
Paul's Third Journey
Bible Passage:
Acts 18:1-4,24-28; 20:17-38
Main Point:
God helped Paul preach with courage.

Paul's Conversion and Baptism

1

BIBLE PASSAGE: Acts 9:1-25

MAIN POINT: Jesus saved Saul from his sins.

KEY PASSAGE: Acts 1:8

BIG PICTURE QUESTION: How do people hear about Jesus? God uses Christians to tell others about Jesus.

INTRODUCE THE STORY
(15–20 MINUTES)
PAGE 98

→

TELL THE STORY
(10–15 MINUTES)
PAGE 100

→

EXPERIENCE THE STORY
(20–25 MINUTES)
PAGE 102

Leader BIBLE STUDY

Saul was no stranger to religion. He grew up in a religious household. He was a devout Jew who was born in Tarsus (Phil. 3:5) and inherited his Roman citizenship from his father. So when people began talking about this man named Jesus and claiming that He was the promised Messiah, Saul was defensive.

Saul believed strongly in the Jewish faith of his ancestors. He violently persecuted God's church and tried to destroy it. (Gal. 1:13-14) He dragged believers from their houses and put them in prison. He approved of the stoning of Stephen, the first Christian martyr. Saul thought he was doing the right thing by defending Judaism, but God's purposes could not be stopped.

As Saul was on his way to arrest believers in Damascus, the Lord stopped him in his tracks. Jesus revealed Himself to Saul, and Saul was never the same. He was struck blind and led into Damascus, where a believer named Ananias placed his hands on Saul. Suddenly, Saul could see again. Saul was convinced that Jesus is Lord. Saul later described the experience as being like dying and receiving a new life. (Gal. 2:20; 2 Cor. 5:17)

God had a purpose and a plan for Saul. He had set Saul apart before Saul was even born. (Gal. 1:15) God said, "This man is My chosen instrument to take My name to the Gentiles" (Acts 9:15).

Jesus changed Saul's life. As you teach preschoolers, clarify that conversion happens when a person recognizes his sin, repents, believes in Jesus, and confesses Jesus as Savior and Lord. Jesus changes a person's heart, and as a result, his life is changed too.

Jesus appeared to Saul and changed him inside and out. Jesus called Saul, who was once an enemy of Christians, to spend the rest of his life telling people the gospel and leading them to trust Jesus as Lord and Savior.

MINISTRY GRID
training made simple

Additional resources for each session are available at *gospelproject.com*. For free training and session-by-session help, visit *www.ministrygrid.com/web/thegospelproject*.

The BIBLE STORY

Paul's Conversion and Baptism

Acts 9:1-25

• **Act it out:** Invite the preschoolers to close their eyes for part of the story. Ask them what it was like to not be able to see.

• **Use lighting:** Enlist another leader to dim the lights and flash a bright light at the appropriate moment in the Bible story.

In the early days of the church, **a man named Saul worked hard to stop people from telling about Jesus. He did not believe that Jesus is the Son of God.** He thought that people who believed in Jesus should be put in jail or be killed. Many believers left the city to get away from Saul.

Saul decided to go to the city of Damascus (duh MASS kuhs) to arrest believers there. He **was traveling** along **when** all of a sudden, **a very bright light came down from heaven. It flashed around Saul, and he fell to the ground. Then Saul heard a voice saying, "Saul, Saul, why are you against Me?"**

"Who are You, Lord?" Saul asked.

"I am Jesus," He said. Jesus told Saul to go into the city and wait for more instructions.

Saul got up and opened his eyes, but **he couldn't see anything! So the men who were traveling with Saul led him into the city.**

A man named Ananias (an uh NIGH uhs) lived in the city. Ananias **loved Jesus. God** spoke to Ananias in a vision and **told him to go visit Saul.** Ananias knew that Saul was an enemy of Jesus, but God had a plan for Saul. **God said, "I have chosen Saul to tell many people about Me."**

Ananias obeyed God. He **went to Saul and said, "Jesus sent me here to help you." Then Ananias put his hands on Saul, and Saul could see again. Saul got up and was baptized.**

For the next few days, **Saul** stayed in the city with other people who believed in Jesus. He **went to the synagogues** to tell people about Jesus. **"Jesus is the Son of God!" Saul** said. The people were amazed. They knew Saul had been an enemy of Jesus, but now he loved Jesus!

The Jews did not like what Saul was saying, so they made a plan to kill him. The other believers helped Saul sneak out of the city at night.

Later, Saul started using the name Paul.

Christ Connection: Saul was an enemy of Jesus and His followers, but then God changed him. Jesus came to earth to save sinners like Paul. (1 Timothy 1:15). When we trust in Jesus, He changes us from the inside out.

WANT TO DISCOVER GOD'S WORD? GET *MORE!*

Invite preschoolers to check out this week's devotionals to discover how God's Word can help them grow in the gospel. Order in bulk, subscribe quarterly, or purchase individually. For more information, check out *www.lifeway.com/devotionals.*

Introduce THE STORY

SESSION TITLE: Paul's Conversion and Baptism

BIBLE PASSAGE: Acts 9:1-25

MAIN POINT: Jesus saved Saul from his sins.

KEY PASSAGE: Acts 1:8

BIG PICTURE QUESTION: How do people hear about Jesus? God uses Christians to tell others about Jesus.

Welcome time

- "Children of the Kingdom" song
- offering basket
- Allergy Alert download
- favorite toys related to the Bible story theme

Play the unit theme song in the background as you greet preschoolers and follow your church's security procedures. Set an offering basket near the door to collect at an appropriate time. Post an allergy alert, if necessary. Set out a few favorite theme-related toys, such as puzzles and blocks.

Activity page

- "Things that Change" activity page, 1 per child
- pencils or crayons

Guide preschoolers to draw a line connecting the thing(s) on the left to what the thing changes into on the right.

SAY • A baby boy changes to become a big boy. An acorn changes to become a tree. Ingredients change to become chocolate chip cookies. A caterpillar changes to become a butterfly. All these things changed on the outside. In today's Bible story, a man named Saul changed on the inside. Listen to our Bible story to hear how God changed Saul.

Play a stop and go game

LOW PREP

- red construction paper
- green construction paper
- marker
- tape

Write *STOP* on a sheet of red construction paper and *GO* on a sheet of green construction paper. Tape the sheets of paper back-to-back so that the words are displayed. Invite preschoolers to line up side by side at one end of the room facing you. When you hold up the GO sign, preschoolers will move toward you. When you hold up the STOP sign, preschoolers must stop in place. Continue flipping between STOP and GO until preschoolers reach you. Allow preschoolers to take turns holding the sign and play again.

SAY • In the early days of the church, a man named Saul worked hard to stop [*hold up the STOP sign*] people from telling about Jesus. He did not believe that Jesus is the Son of God. Many believers left the city to get away from Saul. Even though Saul did not love Jesus, Jesus loved Saul and had a plan for him. Let's discover how Jesus changed Saul in today's Bible story.

Play a voice game

Use an electronic device with an audio recording function to record each preschooler saying a sentence. Be prepared to offer suggested sentences. Play back the recordings to the group and invite preschoolers to guess who is speaking.

• audio recorder

SAY • In today's Bible story, a man named Saul was traveling to the city of Damascus. Someone spoke to Saul while he was traveling along. Saul did not recognize the Person's voice. Let's find out who spoke to Saul in today's Bible story.

Transition to tell the story

To gain the attention of all the preschoolers to move them to Bible study, show the countdown video, flip off the lights, or clap a simple rhythm for the children to copy. Call each child by name to come to Bible study.

• countdown video (optional)

Tell THE STORY

SESSION TITLE: Paul's Conversion and Baptism
BIBLE PASSAGE: Acts 9:1-25
MAIN POINT: Jesus saved Saul from his sins.
KEY PASSAGE: Acts 1:8
BIG PICTURE QUESTION: How do people hear about Jesus? God uses
Christians to tell others about Jesus.

Introduce the Bible story

Ask preschoolers what *saved* means. Give time for responses.
SAY • We talk a lot about "being saved" at church. When
we say Jesus saves someone, we mean that Jesus
rescues that person from sin. We are separated from
God because of our sin, but Jesus died on the cross
to take the punishment for sin. Listen to hear whom
Jesus saved in today's Bible story.

Watch or tell the Bible story

- Bible
- bookmark
- "Paul's Conversion
  and Baptism" video
  (optional)
- Bible Story Picture
  Poster

Place a bookmark at Acts 9 in your Bible. Invite a
preschooler to open it. Reverently display the open Bible.
SAY • God's words are in the Bible, and God's words are true.
Today's Bible story really happened. We find today's
Bible story in the New Testament in the Book of Acts.
Show the video or tell the Bible story using the provided
storytelling helps. Use the bolded version of the Bible story
for young preschoolers.

Talk about the Bible story

- Main Point Poster
- Giant Timeline or
  Big Story Circle

SAY • Saul was Jesus' enemy, but **Jesus saved Saul from his
sins** and Saul changed. Instead of being Jesus' enemy,
now Saul loved Jesus and wanted to tell everyone

about Him.

Point to the Bible story picture on the giant timeline or big story circle as you ask the following review questions:

1. Did Saul love Jesus at the beginning of the Bible story? (*no*)
2. Who spoke to Saul while he was walking to Damascus? (*Jesus*)
3. What happened when Saul opened his eyes after speaking with Jesus? (*He could not see.*)
4. What did Ananias do for Saul? (*put his hands on Saul so he could see again*)
5. Why were the people amazed by Saul? (*They knew he had been an enemy of Jesus, but now he loved Him.*)
6. What was Saul's other name? (*Paul*)

Learn the big picture question

SAY • Our big picture question is, ***How do people hear about Jesus? God uses Christians to tell others about Jesus.*** After **Jesus saved Saul from his sins**, Saul went to the synagogues to tell people about Jesus. God wants us to tell the good news about Jesus to others too.

• Big Picture Question Poster

Practice the key passage

Open your Bible to Acts 1:8. Read the key passage aloud several times. Sing together the key passage song.

SAY • A *witness* tells about what he or she has seen, heard, or experienced. Our key passage tells us that Jesus' followers are His witnesses. We get to tell people what Jesus has done for us!

• Key Passage Poster
• "You Will Be My Witnesses" song

Transition to experience the story

Experience THE STORY

SESSION TITLE: Paul's Conversion and Baptism

BIBLE PASSAGE: Acts 9:1-25

MAIN POINT: Jesus saved Saul from his sins.

KEY PASSAGE: Acts 1:8

BIG PICTURE QUESTION: How do people hear about Jesus? God uses Christians to tell others about Jesus.

Sing a song

Sing the following lyrics to the tune of "Mary had a Little Lamb."

> "Jesus saved Saul from his sins,
> from his sins, from his sins.
> Jesus saved Saul from his sins;
> Jesus was His Lord.
>
> Saul said, 'Jesus is alive,
> is alive, is alive!'
> Saul said, 'Jesus is alive!
> He's the Son of God!'"

SAY • **Jesus saved Saul from his sins.** Saul was an enemy of Jesus and His followers, but then God changed him. Jesus came to earth to save sinners like Paul. When we trust in Jesus, He changes us from the inside out.

Walk blindfolded

• blindfold
• painter's tape

Use painter's tape to make a path. Clear any obstacles. Ask a volunteer to walk the path blindfolded. Choose two other preschoolers to lead the blindfolded preschooler along the path. Ask for a new volunteer and play again. Preschoolers who do not wish to be blindfolded may simply close their eyes.

SAY • Saul could not see anything after Jesus spoke to him on the road. The men who were traveling with Saul led him into the city. Later, Ananias put his hands on Saul, and Saul could see again. **Jesus saved Saul from his sins.** Saul was an enemy of Jesus and His followers, but then God changed him. Jesus came to earth to save sinners like Saul and you and me.

Sequence events

Print and cut apart the "Sequencing Cards" printable. Mix up the cards. Guide preschoolers to arrange the cards in chronological order.

- "Sequencing Cards" printable
- scissors

SAY • **Jesus saved Saul from his sins.** Saul was an enemy of Jesus and His followers, but then God changed him. Jesus came to earth to save sinners like Paul. When we trust in Jesus, He changes us from the inside out.

Experiment with light

Cut out a few circles from black construction paper and post them around the room. Dim the lights. Invite preschoolers to aim the flashlights at the different circles around the room.

Show preschoolers a mirror. Ask them to predict what will happen when they shine the flashlight on the mirror. Demonstrate how the light is reflected to another part of the room when light is shone on a mirror. Show preschoolers how to shift the mirror and the flashlight to

- black construction paper
- scissors
- tape
- flashlights
- nonbreakable mirrors

Tip: Make sure the flashlights you plan to use are strong enough to complete the activity.

move the light around the room. Challenge preschoolers to make the light hit the circles using the mirrors. Make sure preschoolers do not shine light into each other's eyes.

SAY • Saul was traveling along when all of a sudden, a very bright light came down from heaven. It flashed around Saul, and he fell to the ground. **Jesus saved Saul from his sins.** Saul was an enemy of Jesus and His followers, but then God changed him. Jesus came to earth to save sinners like Paul. When we trust in Jesus, He changes us from the inside out.

Dot your name

• paper
• marker
• heavyweight paper
• paint daubers
• pencil

Write *Saul* and *Paul* on separate sheets of paper. Display the signs for preschoolers. Ask children to tell you what is different about the two signs. Remind preschoolers that later Saul started using the name Paul. *Saul* starts with an *S*, and *Paul* starts with a *P*.

Use a pencil to neatly write each child's name on a sheet of heavyweight paper. Invite a preschooler to use a paint dauber to make dots to cover the letters of his name.

SAY • **Jesus saved Saul from his sins.** Jesus told Ananias that He was going to send Saul to tell people about Him. Some places where Saul traveled, he used his other name, Paul. When we trust in Jesus, we usually do not change our names, but Jesus does change us from the inside out. He makes us love Him and other people, and He gives us hearts that want to do what He says.

Snack

Play the countdown video to signal the end of activities. Guide preschoolers to clean their areas. Take a restroom break and wash hands. Gather preschoolers for snack time. Thank God for the snack.

Serve a snack preschoolers may eat with their hands. Remind children that Ananias put his hands on Saul, and Saul could see again. Better than being able to see again, **Jesus saved Saul from his sins.** Saul was an enemy of Jesus and His followers, but then God changed him. Jesus came to earth to save sinners like Paul.

- countdown video (optional)
- Allergy Alert download
- snack food
- paper cups and napkins

Transition

When a child finishes his snack, guide him to throw away any trash. He may select a book or puzzle to examine, play quietly with play dough or a favorite toy, or color the Bible story coloring page.

Offer the journal page and invite preschoolers to draw a picture of themselves. Remind preschoolers that when we trust in Jesus, He changes us from the inside out. Our bodies do not change, but the actions we do with our bodies do. Jesus changes us to love Him and to want to do what He says. Pray for the children.

- books
- puzzles
- play dough
- Journal Page printable, 1 per child
- Bible Story Coloring Page
- crayons
- *Big Picture Cards for Families: Babies, Toddlers, and Preschoolers*

SAY • God, thank You that Jesus came to earth to save sinners like Paul and us. Thank You for changing us when we put our trust in Jesus. Make us love You and others more. Help us to tell others the good news about Jesus. Amen.

If parents are picking up their children at this time, tell them something that their child enjoyed doing or did well during the session. Distribute the preschool big picture cards for families.

Paul's First Journey

BIBLE PASSAGE: Acts 13:1-3; 14:8-28

MAIN POINT: The Holy Spirit sent Paul and Barnabas to tell people about Jesus.

KEY PASSAGE: Acts 1:8

BIG PICTURE QUESTION: How do people hear about Jesus? God uses Christians to tell others about Jesus.

2

INTRODUCE THE STORY (15–20 MINUTES) PAGE 110	TELL THE STORY (10–15 MINUTES) PAGE 112	EXPERIENCE THE STORY (20–25 MINUTES) PAGE 114

 → →

Leader BIBLE STUDY

Jesus' followers preached the gospel in Jerusalem, and the good news spread to places like Judea and Samaria. More and more people believed, and new churches began as both Jews and Gentiles began to follow Jesus. Barnabas went to Antioch—a city about 300 miles north of Jerusalem—where he brought Paul to help teach the believers. The church in Antioch grew. It was in Antioch that the disciples first became known as Christians. (See Acts 11:26.)

The Holy Spirit told the believers at the church in Antioch to send out Paul and Barnabas to preach the gospel. The church obeyed, and Paul and Barnabas traveled to several cities and all over the island of Cyprus, telling both Jews and Gentiles about Jesus.

Consider Paul—once a devoted persecutor of Christians—now a Christian missionary, devoted to obeying God's call to go and tell others the good news about Jesus. This was Paul's first missionary journey, and it wasn't easy. Paul and Barnabas faced rejection in every place that they traveled. Some of the people believed, but some of them were angry. Many people rejected the truth about Jesus. In some places, the Jews made plans to kill Paul.

In no place did Paul and Barnabas soften their message or abandon their mission. In Lystra, Paul healed a man, and when the witnesses to this miracle began to worship Paul and Barnabas, the two men emphatically gave credit to the one true God. When Paul's enemies attacked him and left him for dead, Paul continued on. Paul and Barnabas shared the gospel in Derbe (DUHR bih), and many people believed.

The Holy Spirit sent Paul and Barnabas to tell Jews and Gentiles about Jesus. If Paul had not taken the gospel to the Gentiles, many of us would probably not be believers today. God uses people to tell others about Jesus so that people all over the world can be saved from their sin by trusting in Jesus as Lord and Savior.

MINISTRY GRID
training made simple

Additional resources for each session are available at *gospelproject.com*. For free training and session-by-session help, visit *www.ministrygrid.com/web/thegospelproject*.

The BIBLE STORY

Bible Storytelling Tips

- **Move with the story:** Designate three areas of the room to be Antioch, Lystra, and Derbe. Tell the parts of the story that take place in each city in those different parts of the room, directing the children to travel to the next area of the room before continuing the story.
- **Display a map:** Show a map of Paul's missionary journeys. Trace Paul's first journey as you tell the Bible story.

Paul's First Journey
Acts 13:1-3; 14:8-28

Paul and his friend Barnabas helped start the first churches. The Holy Spirit told Paul and Barnabas that they had a big job to do. **The church put their hands on Paul and Barnabas and prayed for them**, and they left their city to go do the work God wanted them to do. **God led Paul and Barnabas to other cities to tell the good news about Jesus** to both Jews and non-Jews.

Paul and Barnabas went to the city of Lystra (LISS truh). **A man was there who had not been able to walk his whole life.** He listened to Paul talking about Jesus. **Paul saw the man and said in a loud voice, "Stand up!" The man jumped up and began walking around! The people** saw this miracle, and they **thought Paul and Barnabas were gods!** Paul and Barnabas shouted, "No! We are not gods. We are men just like you. We want to tell you the good news of God."

Then **some Jews** came from the other cities Paul and Barnabas had visited. They **made trouble** in this new city, **and the people decided to fight against Paul and Barnabas** too. They threw rocks at Paul and dragged him out of the city.

The next day, Paul and Barnabas went to the city of Derbe (DUHR bih). **They told the people about Jesus, and many of them believed. Finally, they returned to the church and told the other believers** everything that God had done on their journey and how **God helped them share the good news about Jesus with everyone.**

Christ Connection: Paul obeyed the Holy Spirit and shared the gospel with anyone who would listen. People tried to stop Paul, but Paul did not give up. Many people believed in Jesus, and the church grew. The Holy Spirit wants us to tell others about Jesus so they can be saved from their sin.

WANT TO DISCOVER GOD'S WORD? GET *MORE!*

Invite preschoolers to check out this week's devotionals to discover how God's Word can help them grow in the gospel. Order in bulk, subscribe quarterly, or purchase individually. For more information, check out *www.lifeway.com/devotionals.*

Introduce THE STORY

SESSION TITLE: Paul's First Journey

BIBLE PASSAGE: Acts 13:1-3; 14:8-28

MAIN POINT: The Holy Spirit sent Paul and Barnabas to tell people about Jesus.

KEY PASSAGE: Acts 1:8

BIG PICTURE QUESTION: How do people hear about Jesus? God uses Christians to tell others about Jesus.

Welcome time

- "Children of the Kingdom" song
- offering basket
- Allergy Alert download
- favorite toys related to the Bible story theme

Play the unit theme song in the background as you greet preschoolers and follow your church's security procedures. Set an offering basket near the door to collect at an appropriate time. Post an allergy alert, if necessary. Set out a few favorite theme-related toys, such as puzzles and blocks.

Activity page

- "Shadow Matching" activity page, 1 per child
- pencils or crayons

Guide preschoolers to draw a line connecting each transportation vehicle with its shadow.

SAY • What do we use airplanes, boats, cars, and trains to do? [*Allow responses.*] To travel or go from one place to another! In today's Bible story, Paul and his friend Barnabas traveled to different cities to share the gospel, the good news about Jesus.

Sing "I Am a C-H-R-I-S-T-I-A-N"

Lead preschoolers in singing the song "I Am a C-H-R-I-S-T-I-A-N" several times through. Guide preschoolers to move one arm up and down the first time they sing, both arms the second time, two arms and a leg the third time, both arms and both legs the fourth time, and both arms, both legs, and their head the fifth time. Do not emphasize preschoolers singing the song perfectly. Let them have fun trying to sing as they move.

"I am a C
I am a C-H
I am a C-H-R-I-S-T-I-A-N
and I have C-H-R-I-S-T
in my H-E-A-R-T
and I will L-I-V-E E-T-E-R-N-A-L-L-Y!"

If you are unfamiliar with the tune, look it up online before the session.

SAY • C-H-R-I-S-T-I-A-N spells *Christian.* Followers of Jesus were first called Christians in Antioch. The people at the church in Antioch put their hands on Paul and Barnabas and prayed for them. God had given them a special job to do. Let's hear about it in our Bible story.

Walk a sensory path

Use various materials you have on hand to create a path for preschoolers to walk barefoot.

SAY • In today's Bible story, Paul and Barnabas traveled to different cities to tell the good news about Jesus to many people. They did a lot of walking!

• various items, such as a pillow, wet paper, dried beans, bubble wrap, sand, a wooden board, clear contact plastic, cooked noodles

Tip: Avoid materials sticking to feet by placing wet items later in the path.

Transition to tell the story

To gain the attention of all the preschoolers to move them to Bible study, show the countdown video, flip off the lights, or clap a simple rhythm for the children to copy. Invite preschoolers to pretend to be traveling a long distance as they move to Bible study.

• countdown video (optional)

Tell THE STORY

SESSION TITLE: Paul's First Journey

BIBLE PASSAGE: Acts 13:1-3; 14:8-28

MAIN POINT: The Holy Spirit sent Paul and Barnabas to tell people about Jesus.

KEY PASSAGE: Acts 1:8

BIG PICTURE QUESTION: How do people hear about Jesus? God uses Christians to tell others about Jesus.

Introduce the Bible story

Suggested tasks:
- touch your toes
- hop on one foot
- pat your head and rub your tummy at the same time
- touch your nose with your tongue

Instruct preschoolers to perform certain tasks. After each task, ask if completing the task was easy or hard.

SAY • In today's Bible story, Paul and Barnabas shared the gospel with anyone who would listen. Sometimes it was hard. People tried to stop Paul, but Paul did not give up. Listen to what happened.

Watch or tell the Bible story

- Bible
- bookmark
- "Paul's First Journey" video (optional)
- Bible Story Picture Poster

Place a bookmark at Acts 13 in your Bible. Invite a preschooler to open it. Reverently display the open Bible.

SAY • God is so kind to give us His words in the Bible. What the Bible says is true! Today's Bible story happened in real life. We read about it in the Book of Acts.

Show the video or tell the Bible story using the provided storytelling helps. Use the bolded version of the Bible story for young preschoolers.

Talk about the Bible story

- Main Point Poster
- Giant Timeline or Big Story Circle

SAY • Paul and Barnabas helped start the first churches. **The Holy Spirit sent Paul and Barnabas to tell people about Jesus.** It was not always easy. Often

times it was very hard, but the Holy Spirit helped
Paul and Barnabas. They saw many people believe
the good news about Jesus, and the church grew.
Point to the Bible story picture on the giant timeline or big
story circle as you ask the following review questions:
1. Who helped start the first churches? (*Paul and
   Barnabas*)
2. What happened when Paul told the man in Lystra to
   stand up? (*He jumped up and began walking around.*)
3. What did Paul and Barnabas say when the people
   thought they were gods? (*"We are men just like you."*)
4. What did Paul and Barnabas want to tell everyone
   they met? (*the good news about Jesus*)

Learn the big picture question

SAY • Paul obeyed the Holy Spirit and shared the gospel
with anyone who would listen. Many people believed
in Jesus, and the church grew. The Holy Spirit wants
us to tell others about Jesus so they can be saved
from their sin. ***How do people hear about Jesus?
God uses Christians to tell others about Jesus.*** God
wants the good news to spread through people!

• Big Picture Question
Poster

Practice the key passage

Open your Bible to Acts 1:8. Read the key passage aloud
several times. Sing together the key passage song.

SAY • Jesus was talking to His followers when He said
today's key passage. We are Jesus' witnesses. That
means we get to tell others what Jesus has done for us
in His living, dying, and coming back to life!

• Key Passage Poster
• "You Will Be My
Witnesses" song

Transition to experience the story

Experience THE STORY

SESSION TITLE: Paul's First Journey

BIBLE PASSAGE: Acts 13:1-3; 14:8-28

MAIN POINT: The Holy Spirit sent Paul and Barnabas to tell people about Jesus.

KEY PASSAGE: Acts 1:8

BIG PICTURE QUESTION: How do people hear about Jesus? God uses Christians to tell others about Jesus.

Stand up, sit down, walk around

Explain to preschoolers that you will give them three commands: stand up, sit down, and walk around. For each command, preschoolers should perform the following action:

- Stand up: stand tall with arms at sides
- Sit down: sit on the floor with crossed legs and hands folded in lap
- Walk around: march with knees up and arms pumping

Give the commands in varying speeds and order.

SAY • **The Holy Spirit sent Paul and Barnabas to tell people about Jesus.** In Lystra, they met a man who had never been able to walk. They told him to stand up, and he did. It was a miracle! Then Paul and Barnabas told the people in Lystra about Jesus. Many people believed in Jesus, and the church grew.

Play out packing for a trip

- suitcases
- duffel bags
- toiletry bags
- laundry baskets
- clothing items
- empty toiletry bottles
- pillows

Set out suitcases, duffel bags, and toiletry bags. Fill laundry baskets with clothing items, pillows, and empty toiletry bottles. Invite preschoolers to play out packing for a trip by searching through the baskets and placing items into the travel bags. Show children how to fold different items of clothing to fit into a suitcase.

SAY • Paul and Barnabas left their city to share the gospel with people in other cities. What do you think Paul and Barnabas took with them on their trip? **The Holy Spirit sent Paul and Barnabas to tell people about Jesus.** Paul obeyed the Holy Spirit and many people believed in Jesus. The church grew.

Make finger puppets

Print a "Finger Puppets" printable onto heavyweight paper for each preschooler. Before the session, cut out the puppets along the dotted cut lines. Cut out the finger holes using a craft knife. Invite preschoolers to color their puppet images. Show a preschooler how to push his index finger and middle finger through the finger holes to serve as a puppet's legs. Invite preschoolers to use their puppets to play out the Bible story.

- "Finger Puppets" printables, 1 per child
- craft knife (adult use only)
- markers or crayons
- blunt-tipped scissors

SAY • **The Holy Spirit sent Paul and Barnabas to tell people about Jesus.** After Paul healed the man who could not walk, the people thought Paul and Barnabas were gods! But Paul and Barnabas were ordinary people like you and me. The Holy Spirit gave them power, and He gives us power too. The Holy Spirit wants us to tell others about Jesus so they can be save from their sin.

Invite a missionary to class

Invite to your class a missionary your church supports or a church member who has gone on a mission trip or is going on a mission trip. Ask him to share about the work he does

- guest

and the place where he serves. Consider playing a game, sampling a food, or singing a song common to the people group served. Consider leading preschoolers to lay their hands on the guest and pray for him.

SAY • Just like **the Holy Spirit sent Paul and Barnabas to tell people about Jesus**, the Holy Spirit sent [*guest's name*] to tell the good news about Jesus with other people. The Holy Spirit wants us to share the gospel with others so they can be saved from their sin, too. The Holy Spirit may send you to another place to tell the good news one day, but you can tell people the good news right now, right where you live. Whom can you tell?

Clip clothespins on a box

• rigid boxes, 3
• scissors
• marker
• clothespins

Remove the lids from three rigid boxes. Label the boxes as *Antioch*, *Lystra*, and *Derbe*. Draw Bible times buildings under the labels to help preschoolers identify those words as different cities. Draw various colored dots along the ridges of the boxes. Use the same colors to draw stick figures on the clothespins. Invite a preschooler to clip a clothespin with the corresponding colored stick figure on the appropriate dot.

SAY • As Paul and Barnabas shared the gospel, the good news about Jesus, many people believed and the church grew. **The Holy Spirit sent Paul and Barnabas to tell people about Jesus.** Paul obeyed the Holy Spirit and shared the gospel with anyone who would listen. People tried to stop Paul, but Paul did not give up. The church is still growing today. The Holy Spirit uses believers like us to tell others about Jesus so they can be saved from their sin.

Snack

Play the countdown video to signal the end of activities. Guide preschoolers to clean their areas. Take a restroom break and wash hands. Gather preschoolers for snack time. Thank God for the snack.

Serve trail mix for snack. Explain that trail mix gets its name because it is good to eat when you are walking a long time. Remind preschoolers that Paul and Barnabas traveled long distances to share the gospel with anyone who would listen. ***How do people hear about Jesus? God uses Christians to tell others about Jesus.*** The Holy Spirit wants us to tell others about Jesus so they can be saved from sin.

- countdown video (optional)
- Allergy Alert download
- snack food
- paper cups and napkins

Transition

When a child finishes her snack, guide her to throw away any trash. She may select a book or puzzle to examine, play quietly with play dough or a favorite toy, or color the Bible story coloring page.

Offer the journal page and invite preschoolers to draw a picture of a place where they can tell someone about Jesus. Point out that any place is a good place to tell someone the good news. We can listen to the Holy Spirit as He guides us. Pray for the children.

- books
- puzzles
- play dough
- Journal Page printable, 1 per child
- Bible Story Coloring Page
- crayons
- *Big Picture Cards for Families: Babies, Toddlers, and Preschoolers*

SAY • God, make us bold to share the gospel with anyone who will listen. Help us to never give up. Help us listen to the Holy Spirit when He leads us. Thank You for sending Jesus to save us from sin. Amen.

If parents are picking up their children at this time, tell them something that their child enjoyed doing or did well during the session. Distribute the preschool big picture cards for families.

The Message: "Christ Alone"

BIBLE PASSAGE: Acts 15:1-35

MAIN POINT: The church encouraged Gentile believers.

KEY PASSAGE: Acts 1:8

BIG PICTURE QUESTION: How do people hear about Jesus? God uses Christians to tell others about Jesus.

INTRODUCE THE STORY	TELL THE STORY	EXPERIENCE THE STORY
(15–20 MINUTES)	(10–15 MINUTES)	(20–25 MINUTES)
PAGE 122	PAGE 124	PAGE 126

 → →

Leader BIBLE STUDY

The church in Antioch praised God for His grace to Paul on his first missionary journey. Though Paul and Barnabas were strongly opposed in some places, many people heard the gospel and believed. Paul and Barnabas took the gospel to both Jews and Gentiles. But a problem arose when some Christians began saying that the new followers of Jesus—the Gentile believers—needed to obey the Law of Moses in order to be right with God.

Paul and Barnabas debated this issue with other church leaders in Jerusalem. They met together to answer a tough question: Can a person be saved by faith alone or was something more needed? When Paul addressed the council, he insisted that God saves Gentiles the same way He saves Jews: through the grace of the Lord Jesus.

Paul testified to the things God had done among the Gentiles. God had given Gentiles the Holy Spirit. James cited the prophets Amos and Isaiah in support. The group agreed that because of Jesus' death and resurrection, He alone is all we need to be saved. They also agreed that they should not make salvation more difficult for Gentiles by adding unnecessary rules.

The church chose two men—Judas and Silas—to go with Paul and Barnabas to the church at Antioch. They wrote a letter for the Gentile believers there, encouraging them and giving them instructions for how to live as followers of Christ.

The message for the Gentile believers was important: Whether Jew or Gentile, salvation comes only through faith in Christ. No one is saved by the law but by grace alone. Emphasize to the preschoolers you teach that, while the Bible does give us plenty of instruction for how to live, sinners are made right with God only by the grace of Jesus. Salvation is a gift. To receive this gift, Jesus is all we need.

MINISTRY GRID
training made simple

Additional resources for each session are available at *gospelproject.com.* For free training and session-by-session help, visit *www.ministrygrid.com/web/thegospelproject.*

The BIBLE STORY

The Message: "Christ Alone"
Acts 15:1-35

- **Read a letter:** Print a copy of the Bible story, fold it, and slide it into an envelope. Take it out and read it as if reading a letter aloud.
- **Act it out:** Assign volunteers the roles of Paul, Barnabas, Peter, and James. Set up a small lectern or podium. Invite children playing roles to stand at the lectern at the appropriate part in the Bible story.
- **Display a map:** Show a map of Paul's missionary journeys. Point to Jerusalem as you tell the Bible story.

Paul and Barnabas had been teaching people—**Jews and non-Jews**—**about Jesus.** Many people believed, and God's church was growing.

But **some of the people in the church began saying that non-Jews could only be saved if they followed the same rules as the Jews.**

Paul and Barnabas knew this was wrong. They had a meeting with other church leaders to talk about what was true. **Peter** stood up and **told** the leaders **about the Gentiles, the non-Jews, who had believed the good news about Jesus. God had given them the Holy Spirit!**

Peter said that Jews could not obey God's law perfectly, so why should they tell non-Jews to obey perfectly? Jews and non-Jews are saved in the same way: by God's grace.

Everyone listened as Paul and Barnabas talked about how they had seen God save Jews and Gentiles too. Then James showed how the words of the prophets showed that **God wanted to save both Jews and Gentiles. This was God's plan all along.**

So **the church leaders decided to write a letter to the Gentile believers.** The letter told the believers what they should not do now that they were believers.

Paul and Barnabas delivered the letter with Judas and Silas, **and the believers were encouraged.**

Christ Connection: The church leaders met to answer a hard question: Can someone be saved by faith alone? Yes! The early church agreed that Jesus is all we need. Anyone who trusts in Him will be saved.

WANT TO DISCOVER GOD'S WORD? GET *MORE!*

Invite preschoolers to check out this week's devotionals to discover how God's Word can help them grow in the gospel. Order in bulk, subscribe quarterly, or purchase individually. For more information, check out *www.lifeway.com/ devotionals.*

Introduce THE STORY

SESSION TITLE: The Message: "Christ Alone"

BIBLE PASSAGE: Acts 15:1-35

MAIN POINT: The church encouraged Gentile believers.

KEY PASSAGE: Acts 1:8

BIG PICTURE QUESTION: How do people hear about Jesus? God uses Christians to tell others about Jesus.

Welcome time

- "Children of the Kingdom" song
- offering basket
- Allergy Alert download
- favorite toys related to the Bible story theme

Play the unit theme song in the background as you greet preschoolers and follow your church's security procedures. Set an offering basket near the door to collect at an appropriate time. Post an allergy alert, if necessary. Set out a few favorite theme-related toys, such as puzzles and blocks.

Activity page

- "What Will Save Me?" activity page, 1 per child
- pencils or crayons

Guide preschoolers to circle the pictures where a child is making a right choice and to draw an *X* over pictures where a child is making a wrong choice. Ask preschoolers if any of those choices can save them.

SAY • We make wrong choices, and we make right choices, but our choices cannot save us from sin. Only Jesus can save us! Jesus always made the right choice for the right reason. Because Jesus is the only One who ever obeyed God perfectly, He is the only One who can save us. That is what church leaders talked about in today's Bible story.

Make up rules

Invite preschoolers to make up their own rules. Encourage creativity. Suggest rules to get preschoolers thinking. Rules may be silly or serious. Examples of rules include "Share our toys. Eat pizza at every meal. Do not talk when the teacher is talking. Jump up and down on the bed every morning."

SAY • Most rules are good. God's rules are all for our good. They show us how life works best, but rules cannot save a person from sin. Some people in the first churches began saying that non-Jews could only be saved if they followed the same rules as the Jews. Paul and Barnabas knew this was wrong. In today's Bible story, they had a meeting with other church leaders to talk about what was true.

Play out having a meeting

Set out business-style clothes for preschoolers to dress up. Invite preschoolers to gather around a table. Set out a stool or music stand to serve as a lectern. Invite preschoolers to play out having an important meeting.

SAY • When people have something important to talk about, they often have a meeting. In today's Bible story, Paul and Barnabas met with the other church leaders to talk about the most important thing of all—how a person is saved. Listen to hear how they answered the question, Can a person be saved by faith alone?

- business dress-up clothes (suit jackets, sport coats, button-up shirts, scarves, glasses, and so forth)
- stool or music stand
- paper
- non-functioning electronic devices
- toy computers
- notepads
- markers

Transition to tell the story

To gain the attention of all the preschoolers to move them to Bible study, show the countdown video, flip off the lights, or clap a simple rhythm for the children to copy. Ask each preschooler "Can someone be saved by faith alone?" as they move to Bible study. Challenge each child to answer with his or her loudest "Yes!"

- countdown video (optional)

Tell THE STORY

SESSION TITLE: The Message: "Christ Alone"
BIBLE PASSAGE: Acts 15:1-35
MAIN POINT: The church encouraged Gentile believers.
KEY PASSAGE: Acts 1:8
BIG PICTURE QUESTION: How do people hear about Jesus? God uses Christians to tell others about Jesus.

Introduce the Bible story

- wrapped gift

Tip: Place a cross figure or cutout in the box for preschoolers who will be concerned with what is in the gift.

Show preschoolers a wrapped gift.

SAY • A gift is not something you work for or earn. Life forever with God is a gift. We cannot earn it. Jesus is all we need to receive this gift. He did everything needed to save us from sin when He died on the cross and rose again. The church leaders talked about this in today's Bible story.

Watch or tell the Bible story

- Bible
- bookmark
- "The Message: Christ Alone" video (optional)
- Bible Story Picture Poster

Place a bookmark at Acts 15 in your Bible. Invite a preschooler to open it. Reverently display the open Bible.

SAY • The Bible tells us everything we need to know about how to be saved. The Bible is God's Word. The Bible is true. Today's Bible story is from the Book of Acts.

Show the video or tell the Bible story using the provided storytelling helps. Use the bolded version of the Bible story for young preschoolers.

Talk about the Bible story

- Main Point Poster
- Giant Timeline or Big Story Circle

SAY • **The church encouraged Gentile believers.** Some people were saying that people had to do more than just believe in Jesus to be saved. They were wrong!

Everyone—no matter who they are—is saved by believing in Jesus only.

Point to the Bible story picture on the giant timeline or big story circle as you ask the following review questions:

1. Whom had Paul and Barnabas been teaching about Jesus? Jews, Gentiles, or both? (*both*)
2. What kind of rules did some people think the Gentiles should follow? (*the same rules as the Jews*)
3. What did God give the Gentiles who believed the good news about Jesus? (*the Holy Spirit*)
4. Can anyone obey God's law perfectly? (*no*)
5. How are both Jews and Gentiles saved? (*by God's grace*)

Learn the big picture question

SAY • Our big picture question is, ***How do people hear about Jesus? God uses Christians to tell others about Jesus.*** Paul, Barnabas, and Peter shared the good news about Jesus with Jews and Gentiles. The good news is for all people. Anyone who trusts in Him will be saved. God wants us to share this message with everyone, too!

• Big Picture Question Poster

Practice the key passage

Open your Bible to Acts 1:8. Read the key passage aloud several times. Sing together the key passage song.

• Key Passage Poster
• "You Will Be My Witnesses" song

SAY • What is *the end of the earth*? [*Allow responses.*] *The end of the earth* means everywhere on earth. Jesus wants all people to hear the good news that He took the punishment for sin and rose again!

Transition to experience the story

The God Who Sends

Experience THE STORY

SESSION TITLE: The Message: "Christ Alone"
BIBLE PASSAGE: Acts 15:1-35
MAIN POINT: The church encouraged Gentile believers.
KEY PASSAGE: Acts 1:8
BIG PICTURE QUESTION: How do people hear about Jesus? God uses Christians to tell others about Jesus.

What can save me?

Invite preschoolers to squat down. Explain that you will call out an action and ask if doing that action can save them. Preschoolers should say, "No," while remaining in a squat. When you say, "Can Jesus save you?" preschoolers should jump up and shout, "Yes! Jesus alone!" Use the following actions or create your own. Intersperse "Can Jesus save you?" throughout as you mention the actions.

- brushing my teeth every day
- praying before I go to bed
- sharing all my toys
- being kind to my little brother or sister
- going to church
- giving food to people who don't have any
- telling other people about Jesus

SAY • All these actions are good things that we should do, but they cannot save us from sin. Jesus is all we need! **The church encouraged Gentile believers.** The church leaders met to answer a hard question: Can someone be saved by faith alone? Yes! Anyone who trusts in Jesus will be saved.

Sing "The B-I-B-L-E"

Lead preschoolers in singing "The B-I-B-L-E." If you are unfamiliar with the tune, look it up online before the session. Consider creating motions for preschoolers to perform as they sing.

> "The B-I-B-L-E
> Yes, that's the book for me!
> I stand alone on the Word of God,
> The B-I-B-L-E!"

Explain to preschoolers that "stand alone on the Word of God" means believing what God says in the Bible is true, not actually standing on a Bible.

SAY • When the church leaders met, James showed how the words the prophets wrote in the Old Testament showed that God wanted to save both Jews and Gentiles. This was God's plan all along! **The church encouraged Gentile believers.** The Bible tells us that anyone who trusts in Jesus will be saved.

"Write" letters to church leaders

Provide paper, crayons or markers, and envelopes. Encourage the preschoolers to "write" letters to give to your church's leaders. Preschoolers may simply draw a picture, scribble, or ask an adult leader to transcribe a message. Write *Thank you for teaching the gospel!* on each letter. Place the letters in envelopes. If possible, deliver the letters to the leaders or leave them in an office where leaders will find them later.

• paper
• crayons or markers
• envelopes

SAY • **The church encouraged Gentile believers.** The church leaders wrote a letter telling them what they should not do now that they were believers. The message of the gospel is the most important message of all! We want to encourage our leaders to keep teaching the truth of the gospel. Jesus is all we need!

Make a cross collage

• heavyweight paper
• blunt-tipped scissors
• magazines and circulars
• glue stick
• self-adhesive labels
• marker or pen

Cut a sheet of heavyweight paper to make a cross shape. Set out an assortment of magazines for preschoolers to look through for pictures of people. Encourage preschoolers to cut out pictures of people and glue them to their cross shapes. Cut out people images before the session for younger preschoolers. Write or print *All people are saved in the same way: by God's grace* on a label to place on each child's artwork.

SAY • The cross reminds us that Jesus did everything needed to save us from sin when He died on the cross and rose again. Can someone be saved by faith alone? Yes! Anyone who trusts in Jesus will be saved. All people are saved in the same way: by God's grace. **The church encouraged Gentile believers.**

Sort items

• sorting items
• muffin pans or bins

Gather a variety of items that are different but similar for preschoolers to sort. Suggested items include various buttons, different colors and sizes of pom-poms, assorted rocks, or foam shapes. Provide bins or muffin pans for preschoolers to sort the items.

SAY • Two things can be different but still the same in an important way. In today's Bible story, Jews and non-Jews, or Gentiles, had different rules. But they were all saved in the same way: by God's grace. The church leaders wrote a letter to the Gentiles explaining what it meant to live like Christians. **The church encouraged Gentile believers.**

Snack

Play the countdown video to signal the end of activities. Guide preschoolers to clean their areas. Take a restroom break and wash hands. Gather preschoolers for snack time. Thank God for the snack.

Serve pretzel sticks for snack. Encourage preschoolers to use their pretzels to form a cross. Remind preschoolers that the message of the cross is that Jesus died to take the punishment for sin. Jesus rose again to show that He had done all that was needed to save us. The message of the cross is the most important message of all. The church leaders were right to protect it. **The church encouraged Gentile believers.**

- countdown video (optional)
- Allergy Alert download
- snack food
- paper cups and napkins

Transition

When a child finishes his snack, guide him to throw away any trash. He may select a book or puzzle to examine, play quietly with play dough or a favorite toy, or color the Bible story coloring page.

Offer the journal page and invite preschoolers to draw a picture of the cross. Remind preschoolers that there is nothing they can do to save themselves. Jesus is all we need. Anyone who trusts in Him will be saved. Pray for the children.

- books
- puzzles
- play dough
- Journal Page printable, 1 per child
- Bible Story Coloring Page
- crayons
- Big Picture Cards for Families: Babies, Toddlers, and Preschoolers

SAY • God, You gave Your very own Son to save people from sin. We do not have to try really hard to make You love us. You love us because You love Your Son. Help us to put all our trust in Him! Amen.

If parents are picking up their children at this time, tell them something that their child enjoyed doing or did well during the session. Distribute the preschool big picture cards for families.

Paul's Second Journey

BIBLE PASSAGE: Acts 16:11-34
MAIN POINT: Paul and Silas told all kinds of people about Jesus.
KEY PASSAGE: Acts 1:8
BIG PICTURE QUESTION: How do people hear about Jesus? God uses Christians to tell others about Jesus.

INTRODUCE THE STORY
(15–20 MINUTES)
PAGE 134

TELL THE STORY
(10–15 MINUTES)
PAGE 136

EXPERIENCE THE STORY
(20–25 MINUTES)
PAGE 138

 → →

4

Leader BIBLE STUDY

Paul was back at the church of Antioch in Syria. The church had sent out Paul and Barnabas to preach the gospel to Jews and Gentiles in places like Lystra and Derbe. Then they returned to the church of Antioch. Some time passed, and Paul wanted to return to some of the cities he visited on his first journey to see how the new believers were doing.

Silas accompanied Paul on his second missionary journey. The pair traveled through Syria and Cilicia (sih LISH ih uh), encouraging believers and strengthening churches. The number of believers in the churches increased daily.

The Lord called Paul and Silas to go to Macedonia, so they obeyed. Two major events happened while Paul was in Macedonia. First, a woman named Lydia became a believer. Paul and Silas had gone to the river to pray. They spoke to the women at the river. God opened Lydia's heart to the good news of the gospel.

Then, a jailer became a believer. This happened when Paul and Silas were thrown into prison after Paul commanded a fortune-telling spirit to come out of a slave girl. Late at night, an earthquake rocked the prison. The prisoners could have escaped, but they stayed where they were.

This was a huge relief to the jailer. Had the prisoners escaped, the jailer would have been punished. In fact, the jailer was ready to kill himself when Paul shouted, "We are all here!" The jailer asked Paul and Silas how to be saved. They told him, "Believe in the Lord Jesus, and you will be saved." The man believed and was baptized.

4

Lydia, the jailer, and many others were saved because they heard the gospel and believed in Jesus. Paul and Silas preached the same message to all people, no matter who they were: "Believe in the Lord Jesus and you will be saved."

MINISTRY GRID
training made simple

Additional resources for each session are available at *gospelproject.com*. For free training and session-by-session help, visit *www.ministrygrid.com/web/thegospelproject*.

The God Who Sends

The BIBLE STORY

Paul's Second Journey

Acts 16:11-34

• **Display a map:**
Show a map of Paul's missionary journeys. Trace Paul's second journey as you tell the Bible story.

• **Use images:** Print and cut out the "Bible Story People" images on heavyweight paper. Place tape on the back of the Paul and Barnabas images. On a large sheet of paper or dry erase board, draw a river on the left, a town in the middle, and a jail on the right. Move Paul and Silas to those different places as you tell the Bible story.

God sent Paul on another trip to tell people **the good news about Jesus.** This time, **Paul's friend Silas** (SIGH luhs) **went too. Paul stopped in a city** called Philippi (FIH lih pigh), **and** he **went to the river to pray. Paul talked to some women there. One of the women was named Lydia.** She sold purple cloth. **Lydia believed what Paul said about Jesus. Everyone in her household believed, and they were baptized.**

Another day, Paul and Silas were going to pray when a servant girl met them. She had a spirit in her that allowed her to predict the future. She earned a lot of money for her masters by telling the future.

The girl followed Paul and Silas, shouting, "These men are servants of the Most High God!" Finally, **Paul** turned around. He **spoke to the spirit: "By the power of Jesus Christ, I command you to come out of her!" And the spirit came out** right away.

Now **the girl's owners** were upset because she could no longer tell the future. They **grabbed Paul and Silas, and the leaders threw them into jail.**

About midnight, **Paul and Silas were praying and singing songs to God.** All of a sudden, **an earthquake shook the jail. The jail doors flew open, and all of the prisoners' chains came loose.**

When **the jailer** woke up and **thought all the prisoners had escaped,** Paul shouted, "We are all here!"

The jailer was afraid. "Men, what must I do to be saved?" he asked.

They said to him, "Believe in the Lord Jesus and you

will be saved."

Paul and Silas told the jailer and everyone in his household about Jesus, and they were baptized right away. **Later that day, Paul and Silas were set free.**

Christ Connection: Lydia, the jailer, and many others believed in Jesus and were saved from their sin. Paul and Silas told everyone the same thing: "Believe in the Lord Jesus and you will be saved."

WANT TO DISCOVER GOD'S WORD? GET *MORE!*

Invite preschoolers to check out this week's devotionals to discover how God's Word can help them grow in the gospel. Order in bulk, subscribe quarterly, or purchase individually. For more information, check out *www.lifeway.com/devotionals.*

Introduce THE STORY

SESSION TITLE: Paul's Second Journey
BIBLE PASSAGE: Acts 16:11-34
MAIN POINT: Paul and Silas told all kinds of people about Jesus.
KEY PASSAGE: Acts 1:8
BIG PICTURE QUESTION: How do people hear about Jesus? God uses Christians to tell others about Jesus.

Welcome time

- "Children of the Kingdom" song
- offering basket
- Allergy Alert download
- favorite toys related to the Bible story theme

Play the unit theme song in the background as you greet preschoolers and follow your church's security procedures. Set an offering basket near the door to collect at an appropriate time. Post an allergy alert, if necessary. Set out a few favorite theme-related toys, such as puzzles and blocks.

Activity page

- "Color by Number" activity page, 1 per child
- colored pencils or crayons

Lead preschoolers to color the sections with a *1* green, the sections with a *2* purple, and the sections with a *3* brown.

SAY • In today's Bible story, God sent Paul on another trip to tell people the good news about Jesus. He went to a river to pray and met some women there. One of the women was named Lydia. She sold purple cloth. Listen to hear if Lydia believed the truth about Jesus.

Sing songs

Play favorite songs and invite preschoolers to sing along and move. Consider offering streamers for preschoolers to wave as they move to the music.

SAY • Singing is fun! We often sing when we are happy. In today's Bible story, Paul and Silas sang songs in a place where you would not expect them to be singing. Listen to our Bible story to find out where Paul and Silas sang.

• "Children of the Kingdom" song (optional)
• "You Will Be My Witnesses" song (optional)
• streamers (optional)

Sort cloth

Cut an assortment of fabrics into pieces. Consider using stained or outdated clothing and linens. Be sure to include a purple fabric. Spread out the cloth pieces and invite preschoolers to sort them into piles or baskets. Consider challenging preschoolers to close their eyes and match the fabrics using their sense of touch.

SAY • A woman in today's Bible story was named Lydia. She sold purple cloth. Lydia met Paul and Silas when they went to the river to pray. Let's find out what happened when Paul and Silas shared the good news about Jesus with Lydia.

• various fabrics (including purple)
• scissors (adult use)
• baskets (optional)

Transition to tell the story

To gain the attention of all the preschoolers to move them to Bible study, show the countdown video, flip off the lights, or clap a simple rhythm for the children to copy. Invite preschoolers to move to Bible study two by two.

• countdown video (optional)

Tell THE STORY

SESSION TITLE: Paul's Second Journey
BIBLE PASSAGE: Acts 16:11-34
MAIN POINT: Paul and Silas told all kinds of people about Jesus.
KEY PASSAGE: Acts 1:8
BIG PICTURE QUESTION: How do people hear about Jesus? God uses
Christians to tell others about Jesus.

Introduce the Bible story

Tell preschoolers the story of how you first met one of the
other adult leaders in the room.
SAY • God sent Paul on many trips where he met many
people. Paul told everyone he met the same thing:
"Believe in the Lord Jesus and you will be saved."
Listen to hear who Paul met in today's Bible story.

Watch or tell the Bible story

• Bible
• bookmark
• "Paul's Second Journey"
  video (optional)
• Bible Story Picture
  Poster

Place a bookmark at Acts 16 in your Bible. Invite a
preschooler to open it. Reverently display the open Bible.
SAY • The stories in the Bible are there because God
wanted us to hear them. All of these stories are true.
Today's story comes from Acts in the New Testament.
Show the video or tell the Bible story using the provided
storytelling helps. Use the bolded version of the Bible story
for young preschoolers.

Talk about the Bible story

• Main Point Poster
• Giant Timeline or
  Big Story Circle

SAY • **Paul and Silas told all kinds of people about
Jesus.** They told the women at the river, and Lydia
believed. They told the jailer who was afraid of losing
his prisoners, and he believed. It was not easy, but

Paul and Silas told everyone who would listen the good news about Jesus.

Point to the Bible story picture on the giant timeline or big story circle as you ask the following review questions:

1. What woman and her family believed the truth about Jesus and were baptized? (*Lydia*)
2. What happened while Paul and Silas were in jail? (*An earthquake opened the doors and loosened the chains.*)
3. Did any of the prisoners escape from jail? (*no*)
4. What did the jailer ask Paul and Silas? (*"What must I do to be saved?"*)
5. Did the jailer believe the good news about Jesus? (*yes*)

Learn the big picture question

SAY • Our big picture question is, ***How do people hear about Jesus? God uses Christians to tell others about Jesus.*** God used Paul and Silas to tell Lydia, the jailer, and many others the good news about Jesus. Paul and Silas told everyone the same thing: "Believe in the Lord Jesus and you will be saved." We can tell people that same message today!

• Big Picture Question Poster

Practice the key passage

Open your Bible to Acts 1:8. Read the key passage aloud several times. Sing together the key passage song.

SAY • Our key passage remind us about the mission, or very important job, Jesus gave to His followers. Our mission is to tell people all over the world the good news that Jesus died and rose again to save people from sin.

• Key Passage Poster
• "You Will Be My Witnesses" song

Transition to experience the story

Experience THE STORY

SESSION TITLE: Paul's Second Journey

BIBLE PASSAGE: Acts 16:11-34

MAIN POINT: Paul and Silas told all kinds of people about Jesus.

KEY PASSAGE: Acts 1:8

BIG PICTURE QUESTION: How do people hear about Jesus? God uses Christians to tell others about Jesus.

Sing a song

Sing the lyrics below to the tune of "London Bridge Is Falling Down" and perform the described actions.

[Two adults face each other and extend the their arms like a bridge. Children walk underneath the "bridge."]

"Preaching Jesus day and night,
Day and night,
Day and night!
Preaching Jesus day and night
Paul and Silas!"

[Bring arms down over children who are under the "bridge."]

"Take the key and lock them up,
Lock them up,
Lock them up!
Take the key and lock them up!
Then at midnight …"

[Release the children who are trapped in the adult arms.]

"All the prisoners' chains came loose,
Chains came loose
Chains came loose!
All the prisoners' chains came loose!
Thank You, Jesus!"

SAY • Paul and Silas were put in jail, but God sent an earthquake to set them free. Even though they were free, they did not leave. They stayed and told the jailer about Jesus. **Paul and Silas told all kinds of people about Jesus.**

Decide "Who Am I?"

Print and display the "Bible Story People" images. Say statements about each person. Invite preschoolers to point to the image of that person. You may use the following statements or create your own.

- I was afraid when I thought all my prisoners had escaped after the earthquake. Paul and Silas told me to believe in Jesus, and I did. Who am I? (*jailer*)
- I traveled with my friend Paul to tell others the good news about Jesus. Who am I? (*Silas*)
- I met Paul and Silas at the river. They told me about Jesus, and I believed. Who am I? (*Lydia*)
- I traveled to many places telling people the truth about Jesus so they could be saved. Who am I? (*Paul*)

SAY • **Paul and Silas told all kinds of people about Jesus.** Lydia, the jailer, and many others believed in Jesus and were saved from their sin. Paul and Silas told everyone the same thing: "Believe in the Lord Jesus and you will be saved."

Make purple paint

Squirt red and blue washable paint onto a foam plate. Invite preschoolers to predict what will happen to the colors when the paints are mixed. Use a craft stick to mix the paints to create purple paint. Give each preschooler a plate with blue and red paint to mix. Provide shaped sponges for children to paint purple shapes onto a sheet of paper.

SAY • **Paul and Silas told all kinds of people about**

• "Bible Story People" printable

• red and blue washable paint
• foam plates
• craft sticks
• shaped sponges
• construction paper

Jesus. One of the people they told was Lydia. Lydia sold purple cloth. Lydia, the jailer, and many others believed in Jesus and were saved from their sin because Paul and Silas shared the truth with them. They told everyone the same thing: "Believe in the Lord Jesus and you will be saved."

Make play dough chains

• play dough
• various chains
  (optional)

Set out play dough. Invite preschoolers to roll pieces of play dough into "worms." Demonstrate how to loop two worms together and pinch the ends to form a chain. Invite preschoolers to continue adding links to the play dough chain. For younger preschoolers, offer plastic chains for children to press into the play dough.

SAY • An earthquake came while Paul and Silas were in jail. The jail doors flew open, and all of the prisoners' chains came loose. The jailer was afraid and asked Paul and Silas what to do to be saved. Paul and Silas told him, "Believe in the Lord Jesus and you will be saved." **Paul and Silas told all kinds of people about Jesus.**

Work transportation puzzles

• transportation puzzles

Set out a variety of puzzles depicting transportation vehicles. Review the Bible story as preschoolers work.

SAY • God sent Paul on many trips to tell people the good news about Jesus. Most of the time Paul walked or sailed in a boat. **Paul and Silas told all kinds of people about Jesus.** Lydia, the jailer, and many others believed in Jesus and were saved from their sin. Paul and Silas told everyone the same thing: "Believe in the Lord Jesus and you will be saved."

Snack

Play the countdown video to signal the end of activities. Guide preschoolers to clean their areas. Take a restroom break and wash hands. Gather preschoolers for snack time. Thank God for the snack.

Serve granola bars for snack. Point out that granola bars are a good snack to take on a trip. Talk about how God sent Paul on different trips to tell people the good news about Jesus. **Paul and Silas told all kinds of people about Jesus.** Lydia, the jailer, and many others believed in Jesus and were saved from their sin. Paul and Silas told everyone the same thing: "Believe in the Lord Jesus and you will be saved."

- countdown video (optional)
- Allergy Alert download
- snack food
- paper cups and napkins

Transition

When a child finishes her snack, guide her to throw away any trash. She may select a book or puzzle to examine, play quietly with play dough or a favorite toy, or color the Bible story coloring page.

Offer the journal page and invite preschoolers to draw a picture of someone they can tell about Jesus. Ask preschoolers, *How do people hear about Jesus? God uses Christians to tell others about Jesus.* God wants us to share the good news about Jesus with all kind of people too. Pray for the children.

- books
- puzzles
- play dough
- Journal Page printable, 1 per child
- Bible Story Coloring Page
- crayons
- *Big Picture Cards for Families: Babies, Toddlers, and Preschoolers*

SAY • God, the good news that Jesus died on the cross and rose again is the best news ever. It is the only news that can save us from sin. Help us to tell everyone about Jesus so they can be saved. Amen.

If parents are picking up their children at this time, tell them something that their child enjoyed doing or did well during the session. Distribute the preschool big picture cards for families.

Paul Preached in Europe

BIBLE PASSAGE: Acts 17:16-34

MAIN POINT: Paul taught the people in Athens about the one true God.

KEY PASSAGE: Acts 1:8

BIG PICTURE QUESTION: How do people hear about Jesus? God uses Christians to tell others about Jesus.

INTRODUCE THE STORY
(15–20 MINUTES)
PAGE 146

TELL THE STORY
(10–15 MINUTES)
PAGE 148

EXPERIENCE THE STORY
(20–25 MINUTES)
PAGE 150

Leader BIBLE STUDY

Paul and Silas had been released from prison in Philippi (FIH lih pigh). Before leaving the city, they met with believers at Lydia's house and encouraged them. Then they traveled to Thessalonica and stopped at the synagogue to explain to the Jews that Jesus is the Messiah. A large number of Greeks and influential women believed in Jesus.

Before long, Jews in the city became jealous and forced Paul and Silas out of the city. Even though the Jews opposed Paul's preaching, the number of believers in Thessalonica grew and the church there was established.

Paul made his way through Berea, where people heard the gospel and believed. The Jews from Thessalonica followed him and caused trouble, so Paul went to Athens. Athens—about 200 miles from Berea—was a cultural center. People in Athens loved to hear about and study the latest ideas. The Jews and the philosophers in the city were interested in what Paul had to say, but Paul was troubled by what he saw. Athens was full of idols to every kind of god. There was even an altar to an unknown god.

The people obviously had a religious desire. Paul knew that their hunger for God could be satisfied—in Jesus. Paul began preaching, telling the people that they worshiped a god they did not know. He said that people can know God! God made the world and everything in it! "We ought not to think that God is like gold or silver or stone, an image formed by the art and imagination of man," Paul said.

Then Paul told them about Jesus and how God wanted them to turn away from their sins. Some people made fun of Paul, but others believed. Paul explained God's plan of salvation. God is not like the Greek idols. Only God deserves our worship! Because Jesus took the punishment for our sin, we can know God.

5

The BIBLE STORY

Bible
Storytelling
Tips

Paul Preached in Europe

Acts 17:16-34

• **Display a map:**
Show a map of Paul's
missionary journeys.
Trace Paul's second
journey as you tell the
Bible story.

• **Use a prop:** Set up
a large cardboard box
beside the teaching
area. Write *unknown
god* on the side of the
box. At the appropriate
part of the Bible story,
draw a big cross over
"unknown god" and
write *Jesus is the one
true God.*

God sent Paul to the city of Athens to tell people
about Jesus. When Paul got there, he was upset! The
people in Athens did not worship the one true God. They
worshiped false gods instead. Paul told the people about
Jesus. He told them that Jesus died and came back to life.
Jesus is alive!

The people wanted to know more. They had an altar
where they worshiped a god they did not know. Paul told
them that he knew who God is. "I will tell you about the
one true God," he said.

Paul said, "God made everything. God made all the
people of the world, and He loves them. God is so big!
God is bigger than any temple. He is not made of gold
or silver or stone. God wants everyone to turn away from
their sin and turn to Him.

Paul said that God sent Jesus to rescue people from
sin. He said Jesus had died and come back to life, and
some of the people laughed. Some people wanted to hear
more later. And some people believed Paul's words, and
they believed in Jesus.

Christ Connection: Paul taught the people in Athens about the one true God. He told them that Jesus died on the cross and is alive! People can know God because Jesus brings us into God's family.

WANT TO DISCOVER GOD'S WORD? GET *MORE!*

Invite preschoolers to check out this week's devotionals to discover how God's Word can help them grow in the gospel. Order in bulk, subscribe quarterly, or purchase individually. For more information, check out *www.lifeway.com/ devotionals.*

Introduce THE STORY

SESSION TITLE: Paul Preached in Europe
BIBLE PASSAGE: Acts 17:16-34
MAIN POINT: Paul taught the people in Athens about the one true God.
KEY PASSAGE: Acts 1:8
BIG PICTURE QUESTION: How do people hear about Jesus? God uses Christians to tell others about Jesus.

Welcome time

- "Children of the Kingdom" song
- offering basket
- Allergy Alert download
- favorite toys related to the Bible story theme

Play the unit theme song in the background as you greet preschoolers and follow your church's security procedures. Set an offering basket near the door to collect at an appropriate time. Post an allergy alert, if necessary. Set out a few favorite theme-related toys, such as puzzles and blocks.

Activity page

- "Paul Goes to Athens" activity page, 1 per child
- pencils or crayons

Invite preschoolers to complete the maze to display Paul's route to Athens.

SAY • God sent Paul to the city of Athens to tell people about Jesus. When Paul got there, he was upset! Listen to today's Bible story to discover what Paul saw that was so upsetting to him.

Make play dough statues

- play dough
- play dough toys

Guide preschoolers to make statues out of play dough. Explain that statues are usually made to look like a person or animal. Often they are the size of the person or animal in real life or even larger. Ask preschoolers to tell you about their statues.

SAY • Statues can be good just to look at or to remind us of someone or something important, but can you imagine worshiping a statue? That sounds silly, doesn't it? In today's Bible story, God sent Paul to the city of Athens. When Paul got there, he was upset! The people in Athens were worshiping false gods! Listen to hear what Paul told the people about the one true God.

Trace feet

Set paper on the floor and invite preschoolers to stand on the paper. Preschoolers may keep their shoes on or remove them. Use a marker or crayon to trace a child's feet. Invite children to use markers or crayons to decorate their footprints.

• paper
• markers or crayons

SAY • Paul used his feet to travel to many different places to share the gospel, the good news about Jesus. God sent Paul to the city of Athens in today's Bible story. Listen to hear what Paul found when he arrived in Athens.

Transition to tell the story

To gain the attention of all the preschoolers to move them to Bible study, show the countdown video, flip off the lights, or clap a simple rhythm for the children to copy. Invite preschoolers to hold up one finger and say, "one true God" as they move to Bible study.

• countdown video
  (optional)

Tell THE STORY

SESSION TITLE: Paul Preached in Europe
BIBLE PASSAGE: Acts 17:16-34
MAIN POINT: Paul taught the people in Athens about the one true God.
KEY PASSAGE: Acts 1:8
BIG PICTURE QUESTION: How do people hear about Jesus? God uses Christians to tell others about Jesus.

Introduce the Bible story

Invite volunteers to tell you what they know about God.

SAY • In today's Bible story, Paul discovered the people of Athens did not know about the one true god. They worshiped false gods! Listen to hear what Paul told them about the one true God and His Son Jesus.

Watch or tell the Bible story

- Bible
- bookmark
- "Paul Preached in Europe" video (optional)
- Bible Story Picture Poster

Place a bookmark at Acts 17 in your Bible. Invite a preschooler to open it. Reverently display the open Bible.

SAY • The Bible is God's Word. Everything in the Bible is true, and it tells us everything we need to know about the one true God. Today's Bible story is found in Acts.

Show the video or tell the Bible story using the provided storytelling helps. Use the bolded version of the Bible story for young preschoolers.

Talk about the Bible story

- Main Point Poster
- Giant Timeline or Big Story Circle

SAY • The people in Athens worshiped false gods. **Paul taught the people in Athens about the one true God.** He told them that the one true God sent Jesus to rescue people from sin. People can know God because Jesus brings us into God's family.

Point to the Bible story picture on the giant timeline or big story circle as you ask the following review questions:

1. Did the people in Athens worship the one true God? (*no*)
2. What did the people of Athens build for a god they did not know? (*an altar*)
3. What did Paul tell the people of Athens about God? (*Answers will vary.*)
4. What did Paul tell the people of Athens about Jesus? (*God sent Jesus to rescue people from sin. Jesus died and came back to life.*)
5. What did the people of Athens think about what Paul told them about Jesus? (*Some laughed, some wanted to hear more, and some believed.*)

Learn the big picture question

SAY • **Paul taught the people in Athens about the one true God.** He told them that Jesus died on the cross and is alive! ***How do people hear about Jesus? God uses Christians to tell others about Jesus.*** God wants us, like Paul, to tell people about Jesus so they can know God and be brought into His family.

• Big Picture Question Poster

Practice the key passage

Open your Bible to Acts 1:8. Read the key passage aloud several times. Sing together the key passage song.

SAY • The gospel, the good news about Jesus, is the most important message of all. Jesus gives us the joy and privilege of taking His message to all people.

• Key Passage Poster
• "You Will Be My Witnesses" song

Transition to experience the story

Experience THE STORY

SESSION TITLE: Paul Preached in Europe

BIBLE PASSAGE: Acts 17:16-34

MAIN POINT: Paul taught the people in Athens about the one true God.

KEY PASSAGE: Acts 1:8

BIG PICTURE QUESTION: How do people hear about Jesus? God uses Christians to tell others about Jesus.

Sing "My God Is So Big"

Lead preschoolers in singing and performing the motions to "My God Is So Big." If you are unfamiliar with the tune or the motions, look them up online before the session.

SAY • **Paul taught the people in Athens about the one true God.** Paul said, "God is so big! God is bigger than any temple." He told them that Jesus died on the cross and is alive! People can know God because Jesus brings us into God's family.

Work puzzles

• puzzles depicting things God made

Set out a variety of puzzles depicting things that God made. Review the Bible story as preschoolers work.

SAY • Paul told the people in Athens that God made everything. God made all the people of the world, and He loves them. **Paul taught the people in Athens about the one true God.** He told them that Jesus died on the cross and is alive! People can know God because Jesus brings us into God's family.

Sort gold, silver, and stone

Before the session, gather small landscape rocks or river rocks. Spray paint some gold, some silver, and leave the others natural. Be sure the painted rocks have thoroughly dried before preschoolers handle them. Set out the "gold, silver, and stone" and invite preschoolers to sort and count them into bins or piles.

- landscape rocks or river rocks
- gold spray paint
- silver spray paint
- bins (optional)

SAY • **Paul taught the people in Athens about the one true God.** He told them that God is not made of gold or silver or stone like their false gods. He told them that Jesus died on the cross and is alive! People can know God because Jesus brings us into God's family. God wants everyone to turn away from sin and trust in His Son, Jesus.

Compare books with the Bible

Set out a variety of books for preschoolers to explore. Include fiction books as well as non-fiction. Place a Bible among the books. As preschoolers browse, comment on how the Bible is different from the other books.

- fiction books
- non-fiction books
- Bible

SAY • **Paul taught the people in Athens about the one true God.** People in Athens loved to hear about and study new ideas. Today, people often read books to learn new things, but there is only one book we can trust completely to tell us what is true about God. That book is the Bible. We can know about the one true God and His Son, Jesus, from the Bible.

Play with transportation toys

- transportation toys (cars, trucks, boats, trains, airplanes)
- blue and black construction paper
- scissors

Set out a variety of transportation toys for preschoolers to play with. Set out strips of black construction paper for preschoolers to use to form roads. The children can use blue sheets of construction paper to form lakes, rivers, and oceans.

SAY • God sent Paul to many different places to share the gospel, the good news about Jesus. **Paul taught the people in Athens about the one true God.** Paul mostly walked or rode in a boat when he traveled. Today, we have lots of different ways we can travel. We can get to many people to tell them that Jesus died on the cross and is alive! People can know God because Jesus brings us into God's family.

Snack

Play the countdown video to signal the end of activities. Guide preschoolers to clean their areas. Take a restroom break and wash hands. Gather preschoolers for snack time. Thank God for the snack.

Serve bread, olives, figs, and cheese for snack. Explain that the people of Athens usually ate foods like these. God loved the people of Athens and wanted them to know about Him and His Son, Jesus. God sent Paul to Athens. **Paul taught the people in Athens about the one true God.** God wants us to tell others about Him too. *How do people hear about Jesus? God uses Christians to tell others about Jesus.*

- countdown video (optional)
- Allergy Alert download
- snack food
- paper cups and napkins

Transition

When a child finishes his snack, guide him to throw away any trash. He may select a book or puzzle to examine, play quietly with play dough or a favorite toy, or color the Bible story coloring page.

Offer the journal page and invite preschoolers to draw a picture of Jesus. Remind preschoolers that Jesus died on the cross and is alive. We can know God because of Jesus. Jesus brings us into God's family. Pray for the children.

SAY • God, thank You that You want people to know You and Your Son, Jesus. Thank You for giving us the mission to share the good news about Jesus with others. Help us tell everyone that Jesus died on the cross and is alive. Amen.

If parents are picking up their children at this time, tell them something that their child enjoyed doing or did well during the session. Distribute the preschool big picture cards for families.

- books
- puzzles
- play dough
- Journal Page printable, 1 per child
- Bible Story Coloring Page
- crayons
- *Big Picture Cards for Families: Babies, Toddlers, and Preschoolers*

Paul's Third Journey

BIBLE PASSAGE: Acts 18:1-4,24-28; 20:17-38
MAIN POINT: God helped Paul preach with courage.
KEY PASSAGE: Acts 1:8
BIG PICTURE QUESTION: How do people hear about Jesus? God uses Christians to tell others about Jesus.

INTRODUCE THE STORY
(15–20 MINUTES)
PAGE 158

TELL THE STORY
(10–15 MINUTES)
PAGE 160

EXPERIENCE THE STORY
(20–25 MINUTES)
PAGE 162

Leader BIBLE STUDY

Paul's third missionary journey was unlike his first two because he didn't set out to plant churches. Instead, his mission was to encourage and strengthen existing churches. Paul wrote letters to the churches, but he knew some guidance was best given in person.

Paul's journey began when he traveled to the city of Corinth. To make a living, Paul was a tentmaker. Paul became friends with two other tentmakers in Corinth: a man named Aquila and his wife, Priscilla. In his business dealings, Paul was able to share the gospel with many people. The church in Corinth grew.

6

Paul took Aquila and Priscilla with him to Ephesus. Ephesus was a thriving city in the Roman Empire. Aquila and Priscilla stayed in Ephesus while Paul traveled to others churches and encouraged the believers. While Paul traveled, Aquila and Priscilla interacted with a Jewish believer named Apollos. Apollos was a leader in the early church, and Aquila and Priscilla helped him better understand about Jesus and the Scriptures. Apollos went on to greatly help other believers by showing through Scripture that Jesus is the Messiah.

The Holy Spirit led Paul to go to Jerusalem. This wasn't an easy call to obey. The Spirit revealed to Paul that imprisonment and suffering awaited in Jerusalem. (See Acts 20:23.) Hadn't Paul done enough? He had spent years preaching the gospel, and many people believed. Wasn't now a good time for Paul to retire comfortably on a beach somewhere?

But Paul did not cling to his own life. He used every opportunity to tell people the good news about Jesus and to help the church. God helped Paul preach with courage even when he was in danger. Paul was dedicated to Jesus, who called him to do the work of sharing the gospel. Paul boarded the ship to Jerusalem, uncertain of the future but certain of the goodness and grace of the Lord Jesus.

6

MINISTRY GRID
training made simple

Additional resources for each session are available at *gospelproject.com*. For free training and session-by-session help, visit *www.ministrygrid.com/web/thegospelproject*.

The BIBLE STORY

Bible Storytelling Tips

Paul's Third Journey
Acts 18:1-4,24-28; 20:17-38

• **Display a map:** Show a map of Paul's missionary journeys. Trace Paul's third journey as you tell the Bible story.

• **Sit in a tent:** Make a tent in the classroom with a sheet. Invite preschoolers to sit in the tent while you tell the Bible story. Remind children that Paul was a tentmaker.

God sent Paul to the city of **Corinth. Paul met a man and his wife, Aquila** (uh KWIL uh) **and Priscilla.** Their job was making tents. Paul made tents too. **Paul stayed with them and worked with them.** On the Sabbath, **Paul went to the synagogue to talk to the people** who lived in the city. He told them **about Jesus. Some of the people believed.** Now the church was in Corinth too.

Paul and his new friends, **Aquila and Priscilla, went to** the city of **Ephesus** (EF uh suhs). **Aquila and Priscilla stayed there, and Paul traveled all around to visit churches.** Paul met with believers at the churches and helped them.

While Paul traveled, a man named Apollos (uh PAHL uhs) **came to Ephesus. Apollos** told people about Jesus. He **knew what was true about Jesus, but he did not understand everything. So Aquila and Priscilla taught him more. Then Apollos traveled and taught more people about Jesus**, and he told them that Jesus is the Messiah.

Now **Paul traveled back toward Ephesus.** He asked the church leaders to meet him nearby. Paul told them that **God wanted him to go to** the city of **Jerusalem.** "I do not know what will happen there," **Paul said,** "but **I know** there will be trouble. **I will be put in prison."**

But this did not stop **Paul.** He **knew** that the most important thing was not having an easy life; **the most important thing was to do the work God had for him.** "I **want to tell people the good news about Jesus,"** he said.

The church leaders prayed with Paul and said goodbye.

Christ Connection: As Paul traveled, he told as many people as he could about Jesus. God changed people's hearts, and the church grew. God called Paul to tell people the good news about Jesus, and Paul wanted to follow God's plan no matter what.

WANT TO DISCOVER GOD'S WORD? GET *MORE!*

Invite preschoolers to check out this week's devotionals to discover how God's Word can help them grow in the gospel. Order in bulk, subscribe quarterly, or purchase individually. For more information, check out *www.lifeway.com/ devotionals.*

Introduce THE STORY

SESSION TITLE: Paul's Third Journey
BIBLE PASSAGE: Acts 18:1-4,24-28; 20:17-38
MAIN POINT: God helped Paul preach with courage.
KEY PASSAGE: Acts 1:8
BIG PICTURE QUESTION: How do people hear about Jesus? God uses Christians to tell others about Jesus.

Welcome time

- "Children of the Kingdom" song
- offering basket
- Allergy Alert download
- favorite toys related to the Bible story theme

Play the unit theme song in the background as you greet preschoolers and follow your church's security procedures. Set an offering basket near the door to collect at an appropriate time. Post an allergy alert, if necessary. Set out a few favorite theme-related toys, such as puzzles and blocks.

Activity page

- "Hidden Picture" activity page, 1 per child
- pencils or crayons

Invite preschoolers to use the key to find the objects hidden in the picture.

SAY • In today's Bible story, Paul continued to travel around encouraging the churches and spreading the gospel, the good news about Jesus. Paul had some hard news to share with the church leaders about where God wanted him to go next. Listen to our Bible story to hear where God was sending Paul and what would be waiting for Paul when he arrived.

Play "Who Is My Friend?"

Explain to preschoolers that you will say a statement describing one of the children in the group. After each statement say, "Who is my friend?" Preschoolers will guess the child you are describing. Say additional statements describing the child until the child is named. Allow older preschoolers to take turns describing their friends.

SAY • God is so kind to give us friends. The best kind of friends are those who follow Jesus, too. Following Jesus is not easy. We need friends who are also believers to encourage us, remind us about Jesus, and help us do the work of spreading the good news. In today's Bible story, Paul learned he was going to have to do something very hard. The other church leaders loved Paul and prayed for him.

Make a tent

Provide large sheets and invite preschoolers to make tents. Preschoolers may simply drape the sheets over chairs or tables. Consider hanging a string between two walls. Make sure the string is secure. Help preschoolers drape a sheet over the string to create a tent. Provide pillows and books to fill the tents.

• large sheets
• string (optional)

SAY • We have been learning a lot about Paul these last few weeks, but did you know that Paul had a job? Paul made tents. In today's Bible story, Paul made some new friends who were also tentmakers. Paul stayed with them and worked with them. Listen for how these new friends helped spread the gospel, the good news about Jesus.

Transition to tell the story

To gain the attention of all the preschoolers to move them to Bible study, show the countdown video, flip off the lights, or clap a simple rhythm for the children to copy. Invite preschooler to give their friends (everyone) high-fives as they move to Bible study.

• countdown video (optional)

Tell THE STORY

SESSION TITLE: Paul's Third Journey
BIBLE PASSAGE: Acts 18:1-4,24-28; 20:17-38
MAIN POINT: God helped Paul preach with courage.
KEY PASSAGE: Acts 1:8
BIG PICTURE QUESTION: How do people hear about Jesus? God uses Christians to tell others about Jesus.

Introduce the Bible story

Define *courage* for preschoolers as being strong when you have to do something very hard or scary.

Tell preschoolers about a time you had to be courageous and how God helped you.

SAY • Courage is different for Christians than for people who are not Christians. God gives us the Holy Spirit. The Holy Spirit gives us courage. We never have to do hard things on our own. Listen to hear how God helped Paul be courageous in today's Bible story.

Watch or tell the Bible story

• Bible
• bookmark
• "Paul's Third Journey" video (optional)
• Bible Story Picture Poster

Place a bookmark at Acts 18 in your Bible. Invite a preschooler to open it. Reverently display the open Bible.

SAY • The Bible is the most special book there is because it has God's words in it. The stories in the Bible really happened. Today's Bible story comes from Acts.

Show the video or tell the Bible story using the provided storytelling helps. Use the bolded version of the Bible story for young preschoolers.

Talk about the Bible story

• Main Point Poster
• Giant Timeline or Big Story Circle

SAY • The good news about Jesus was spreading through many different people. **God helped Paul preach with courage** while he did hard things. Paul knew telling people the good news about Jesus was more important than having an easy life.

Point to the Bible story picture on the giant timeline or big story circle as you ask the following review questions:

1. How did Aquila and Priscilla help Apollos? (*They taught him more about Jesus.*)
2. Where did God want Paul to go? (*Jerusalem*)
3. What would happen to Paul in Jerusalem? (*He would be put in prison.*)
4. What was more important to Paul: having an easy life or doing the work God had for him? (*doing the work God had for him*)
5. What was the work God had for Paul? (*telling people the good news about Jesus*)

Learn the big picture question

SAY • Our big picture question is, ***How do people hear about Jesus? God uses Christians to tell others about Jesus.*** God called Paul to tell people the good news about Jesus, and He calls us to do the same. Telling people about Jesus will sometimes be very hard, but following God's plan is better than having an easy life. Jesus promises to always be with us.

• Big Picture Question Poster

Practice the key passage

Open your Bible to Acts 1:8. Read the key passage aloud several times. Sing together the key passage song.

SAY • Paul was a witness for Jesus. He told as many people as he could about Jesus. We are to be witnesses for Jesus, too, sharing the good news with others.

• Key Passage Poster
• "You Will Be My Witnesses" song

Transition to experience the story

Experience THE STORY

SESSION TITLE: Paul's Third Journey

BIBLE PASSAGE: Acts 18:1-4,24-28; 20:17-38

MAIN POINT: God helped Paul preach with courage.

KEY PASSAGE: Acts 1:8

BIG PICTURE QUESTION: How do people hear about Jesus? God uses Christians to tell others about Jesus.

Play telephone

Play the telephone game. Invite preschoolers to sit in a circle. Whisper in one child's ear a simple truth such as "Jesus is God's Son" or "Jesus died on the cross and is alive." Guide her to tell the truth to the friend on her left. Preschoolers continue telling the good news until every child has heard it.

SAY • Paul traveled and told as many people as he could about Jesus. While Paul traveled, Aquila and Priscilla taught Apollos more about Jesus. Then Apollos traveled and taught more people about Jesus. God changed people's hearts, and the church grew. ***How do people hear about Jesus? God uses Christians to tell others about Jesus.*** God wants to use us to share the good news about Jesus!

Play a review game

• Bible Story Picture Posters for unit 30
• tape
• beanbag

Tape the Bible Story Picture Posters for unit 30 to the floor in a grid. Use tape to create a line on the floor a few feet away from the posters. Lead preschoolers to line up behind the tape line. Invite a preschooler to toss a beanbag toward the posters. Ask him to tell what he remembers from the Bible story depicted in the picture on which the beanbag landed. If the beanbag did not land on a picture, use the poster closest to where it landed.

SAY • We have learned a lot about how God used Paul to take the gospel to many places. **God helped Paul preach with courage.** Paul told as many people as he could about Jesus. God changed people's hearts, and the church grew. God called Paul to tell people the good news about Jesus, and Paul wanted to follow God's plan no matter what.

Make friendship bracelets

Lead preschoolers to cut colorful drinking straws into pieces and string the pieces onto a chenille stem. When a preschooler has finished stringing straw pieces, show her how to twist the ends together to form a bracelet. Be sure sharp edges are bent back. Invite her to give her bracelet to a friend.

- colorful drinking straws
- chenille stems
- blunt-tipped scissors

Tip: Make a bracelet for each preschooler before the session to ensure every child gets a bracelet from a "friend."

SAY • What friend are you going to give your friendship bracelet to? Paul became friends with Priscilla and Aquila in today's Bible story. Then Priscilla and Aquila became friends with Apollos. The church leaders loved Paul and prayed for him. **God helped Paul preach with courage.**

Make cards for Christian prisoners

Identify an organization that ministers to persecuted Christians and distributes letters of encouragement to Christian prisoners. Read and follow the guidelines the organization lays out for sending letters to prisoners.

- construction paper
- stickers
- markers or crayons
- large mailing envelope

Set out construction paper, stickers, and markers or crayons for preschoolers to make and decorate cards. Write "I am praying for you!" on each card. Take time to pray

The God Who Sends

for the prisoners who will receive preschoolers' cards. Place all the cards in a large mailing envelope to mail to the delivering organization.

SAY • God wanted Paul to go to the city of Jerusalem. He knew that he would be put in prison there. **God helped Paul preach with courage.** Paul knew that having an easy life was not the most important thing; the most important thing was to do the work God had for him. Today there are Christians in prison just because they love and follow Jesus. We can pray for them and encourage them.

Float boats

- clean, small plastic containers
- large plastic tub
- towels
- plastic people figures

Gather an assortment of clean, small plastic containers such as yogurt cups, margarine tubs, plastic cups, and so forth. Fill a plastic tub with a few inches of water. Place the tub on a flat surface covered with a towel. Invite preschoolers to experiment to determine which containers float the best and hold the most plastic people figures.

SAY • Paul got on a boat to Jerusalem. Before he got on the boat, the church leaders prayed with him and said goodbye. **God helped Paul preach with courage.** Paul knew that having an easy life was not the most important thing; the most important thing was to do the work God had for him. God called Paul to tell people the good news about Jesus, and Paul wanted to follow God's plan no matter what.

Snack

Play the countdown video to signal the end of activities. Guide preschoolers to clean their areas. Take a restroom break and wash hands. Gather preschoolers for snack time. Thank God for the snack.

Serve graham crackers for snack. Invite preschoolers to lean two graham crackers against each other to form a tent. Remind preschoolers that Paul worked with Aquila and Priscilla making tents. On the Sabbath, Paul went to the synagogue to talk to the people about Jesus. ***How do people hear about Jesus? God uses Christians to tell others about Jesus.*** We may not be able to travel around like Paul, but we can tell people about Jesus right here where we are.

* countdown video (optional)
* Allergy Alert download
* snack food
* paper cups and napkins

Transition

When a child finishes her snack, guide her to throw away any trash. She may select a book or puzzle to examine, play quietly with play dough or a favorite toy, or color the Bible story coloring page.

Offer the journal page and invite preschoolers to draw a picture of a time they can tell someone about Jesus. Sometimes telling people about Jesus is easy, but sometimes it is hard. **God helped Paul preach with courage**, and He will help us too. Pray for the children.

SAY • God, help us to tell as many people as we can about Jesus. Remind us the most important thing is to do the work You have for us. Help us to follow Your plan no matter what. Amen.

If parents are picking up their children at this time, tell them something that their child enjoyed doing or did well during the session. Distribute the preschool big picture cards for families.

* books
* puzzles
* play dough
* Journal Page printable, 1 per child
* Bible Story Coloring Page
* crayons
* Big Picture Cards for Families: Babies, Toddlers, and Preschoolers

5 Mistakes Church Leaders Make in Their Preschool Ministry

A CHURCH'S MINISTRY TO PRESCHOOL CHILDREN IS EXTREMELY IMPORTANT IN BUILDING A STRONG FOUNDATION OF FAITH FOR THE CHILDREN AND IN REACHING AND MINISTERING TO YOUNG FAMILIES.

Preschool ministry is a mission-critical ministry of the church in that it invests in families at a critical juncture in the lives of both parents and children. Because it is so important, it must be close to the heart of those who lead the church. Here are five common mistakes church leaders make with their preschool ministry, mistakes that can give the perception, sometimes accurate, that the leaders do not value the preschool ministry.

#1 Calling it childcare. I am not minimizing childcare. When Kaye and I go on dates, we hand our children to someone we trust who provides excellent care to our kids. It is important. But a preschool ministry is so much more. Children are taught Bible stories, sing songs, and pray together. This is much more than childcare, and calling preschool ministry childcare minimizes the eternal significance of the investment.

#2 Ignoring the facility and bathrooms. Whether in a portable church or a permanent facility, families care if where their children gather and use the bathroom is safe, secure, and clean.

#3 Never thanking those who serve. Those who serve in preschool ministry make a mammoth impact on the young families in your church and guests who visit. They should be thanked and valued.

#4 Never walking around. Ministry leaders—if you never walk around the kids ministry area, it is hard to speak with any authority as to what is happening there.

#5 **Not paying any attention to the length of the service.** I am not advocating for a certain length of your worship services. What I am encouraging, for the sake of the kids ministry, is that they are consistent. If they are inconsistent in length, leaders have a hard time planning and are constantly adjusting. Think about more than just the adult worship service. The adult worship service is not the only place on your church campus where the Lord is working.

Eric Geiger serves as one of the Vice Presidents at LifeWay Christian Resources, leading the Resources Division. Eric has authored or co-authored several books including Creature of the Word and the best selling church leadership book, Simple Church. Eric is married to Kaye, and they have two daughters: Eden and Evie.

Scripture Memory with Kids

THE BIBLE TELLS US THAT MEMORIZATION IS ONE OF THE KEYS TO PUTTING GOD'S WORD IN OUR HEARTS WHERE GOD CAN USE IT TO CHANGE US AND GROW US IN HIS WILL. (PSALM 119:104-105)

We want kids to be able to memorize a Bible verse, put it into practice in their daily lives, and recall it many times throughout their lives. Kids will "treasure" a verse in their hearts and minds when they learn the meaning of the words in a verse; can see a practical, real application of it to their lives; and are exposed to the verse and its truth over and over.

Memorizing Bible verses is so much more than "saying the words by heart." Consider these suggested guidelines:

- Learning that will remain with a child involves more than a one-time use and interpretation of a verse.
- Kids absorb new material gradually. Generally speaking, the younger the child, the fewer the verses he can be expected to learn and relate to his daily life.
- Kids differ in their abilities.

Some kids can memorize words and grasp meanings more quickly.

- Kids are more interested in learning when methods are varied and engaging.
- Kids' learning is enhanced when they are involved in activities such as singing a verse, acting out the meaning of the verse, matching verses with present-day pictures, and activities suitable to the age group.

Teaching Scripture to our kids is an important part of their Christian education. What are you doing to promote Scripture memory in your church?

Bill Emeott serves as Lead Ministry Specialist for LifeWay Kids. A graduate of Mercer University and New Orleans Baptist Theological Seminary. Bill has served as a Kid's Minister and currently teaches 2nd Grade Bible study.

TPS 191627